Alan Titchmarsh
how to garden

Vegetables and Herbs

BBC BOOKS

10 9 8 7 6 5 4 3 2 1

Published in 2009 by BBC Books, an imprint of
Ebury Publishing, a Random House Group Company

The Random House Group Limited Reg. No. 954009

Addresses for companies within the Random House
Group can be found at
www.randomhouse.co.uk

The Random House Group Limited supports The Forest
Stewardship Council (FSC), the leading international
forest certification organisation. All our titles that are
printed on Greenpeace approved FSC certified paper
carry the FSC logo. Our paper procurement policy can
be found at www.rbooks.co.uk/environment

A CIP catalogue record for this book is available from
the British Library.

ISBN 978 1 84 6073960

Produced by Outhouse!
Shalbourne, Marlborough, Wiltshire SN8 3QJ

BBC BOOKS
COMMISSIONING EDITORS: Lorna Russell, Stuart Cooper
PROJECT EDITOR: Caroline McArthur
PRODUCTION CONTROLLER: Bridget Fish

OUTHOUSE!
CONCEPT DEVELOPMENT & PROJECT MANAGEMENT:
   Elizabeth Mallard-Shaw, Sue Gordon
CONTRIBUTING EDITOR: Jo Weeks
PROJECT EDITOR: Bella Pringle
ART DIRECTION: Sharon Cluett
DESIGNER: Sharon Cluett
ILLUSTRATOR: Lizzie Harper

PHOTOGRAPHS by Jonathan Buckley except where
credited otherwise on page 144

Colour origination by Altaimage, London
Printed and bound by Firmengruppe APPL,
Wemdig, Germany

Contents

Introduction

Gardening is one of the best and most fulfilling activities on earth, but it can sometimes seem complicated and confusing. The answers to problems can usually be found in books, but big fat gardening books can be rather daunting. Where do you start? How can you find just the information you want without wading through lots of stuff that is not appropriate to your particular problem? Well, a good index is helpful, but sometimes a smaller book devoted to one particular subject fits the bill better – especially if it is reasonably priced and if you have a small garden where you might not be able to fit in everything suggested in a larger volume.

The *How to Garden* books aim to fill that gap – even if sometimes it may be only a small one. They are clearly set out and written, I hope, in a straightforward, easy-to-understand style. I don't see any point in making gardening complicated, when much of it is based on common sense and observation. (All the key techniques are explained and illustrated, and I've included plenty of tips and tricks of the trade.)

There are suggestions on the best plants and the best varieties to grow in particular situations and for a particular effect. I've tried to keep the information crisp and to the point so that you can find what you need quickly and easily and then put your new-found knowledge into practice. Don't worry if you're not familiar with the Latin names of plants, they are there to make sure you can find the plant as it will be labelled in the nursery or garden centre, but where appropriate I have included common names, too. Forgetting a plant's name need not stand in your way when it comes to being able to grow it.

Above all, the *How to Garden* books are designed to fill you with passion and enthusiasm for your garden and all that its creation and care entails; from designing and planting it to maintaining it and enjoying it. For more than fifty years gardening has been my passion, and that initial enthusiasm for watching plants grow, for trying something new and for just being outside pottering has never faded. If anything I am keener on gardening now than I ever was and get more satisfaction from my plants every day. It's not that I am simply a romantic, but rather that I have learned to look for the good in gardens and in plants, and there is lots to be found. Oh, there are times when I fail – when my plants don't grow as well as they should and I need to try harder. But where would I rather be on a sunny day? Nowhere!

The *How to Garden* handbooks will, I hope, allow some of that enthusiasm – childish though it may be – to rub off on you, and the information they contain will, I hope, make you a better gardener, as well as opening your eyes to the magic of plants and flowers.

Becoming a vegetable gardener

Anyone can grow their own veg. In fact, it's all too easy to get bitten by the veg-gardening bug: perhaps the children want to try growing a few beans or courgettes in a tub; or a neighbour has raised one too many tomato plants and is longing to palm off a couple on you; or you spot a tray of lettuce seedlings at a car boot sale or garden centre. Beware, these little beginnings may ignite a passion that simply grows and grows.

Why grow your own?

Recently there has been a resurgence in vegetable gardening. It is difficult to pinpoint why, but it is probably a combination of factors: getting fed up with the same sterile-looking produce offered in the supermarkets; feeling a need for the tranquillity offered by pootling about in the garden; or realizing that the jet-setting lives led by many of our shop-bought fruit and veg cannot be good for us, them, or the planet. Whatever the reason, growing vegetables brings a multitude of rewards.

Even if you don't have acres of space, you can grow vegetables. For those who have plenty of room, the veg-growing bug can result in an entire garden being given over to edible produce. All power to your potager!

Taste

Nowadays we are used to being able to buy all sorts of vegetables in the shops, all the year round. We can have tomatoes in winter and courgettes in early spring. But where is the taste? All the greenhouse heating and lighting in the world hasn't been able to recreate the wonderful flavour of a home-grown tomato picked and eaten just as it reaches ripe perfection, or a cucumber sliced into a salad while still warm from the greenhouse. The thought of the amazing sweetness of a sweetcorn cob so fresh that it might have been bent over a pan of boiling water while still on the plant, should start to make your mouth water. Or what about the simple pleasure of shelling young peas and broad beans and trying not to eat them all before they reach the colander?

Convenience

Aside from their great taste, there are practical advantages to raising your own vegetables. You can ensure that you have a fresh supply of the family's favourites on your doorstep (or just down the road at the allotment), and you can also save money by growing vegetables that are more expensive to buy,

such as asparagus and artichokes. As you tend them every single day of their lives, you will know exactly what your vegetables have been exposed to in terms of chemicals and other undesirables. While this is particularly important for those of us who have children to feed, it is also nice to know that you aren't putting anything unnecessary into your own body. And while we're on bodies, gardening is excellent exercise, getting you out into the fresh air and toning up muscles you didn't know you had.

Reality check

After all the words in praise of vegetable gardening, a few of warning: it does require commitment. It's no good bunging in a few plants and hoping for the best, you do need to plan, prepare, plant and cherish. It is also important not to be too ambitious – if you have never grown veg before, don't try to be self-sufficient in year one. In fact, unless you really have a bee in your bonnet, it is best to accept that some things are always more sensibly bought at the local greengrocer or supermarket, and to concentrate on those vegetables that are really worth growing at home. And a final spoiler – a lot of gardening is about waiting: if you are reading this in midsummer, you won't see all your dreams come to fruition until next year. The best time to start planning a vegetable patch is in the autumn or winter, so you can do the necessary preparations in time for the start of the growing season in spring.

The owner of this vegetable garden is making the most of his restricted space. Growing vegetable plants in tiers on a sunny wall makes sense because most won't grow higher than 30cm (12in) or so, which means you can fit in plenty of containers. If growing crops in pots, you must pay great attention to feeding and watering.

Planning your plot

If you have the luxury of space in your garden, you will be able to choose a sheltered site, with a good sunny aspect and free-draining soil for growing vegetables. This is the ideal, but some of us who have limited space or are allocated an allotment can plan an equally productive plot by following a few simple rules.

This is a vegetable garden with designer flair. Although it is only a tiny corner, this plot has a greenhouse, compost bin and cloches, as well as a selection of healthy vegetables in raised beds.

Site

Vegetables have to grow fast and steadily to produce an abundant, healthy and tasty crop. To do this they need fertile soil that drains well after rain. They also do best with plenty of sun and water and protection from wind. Keep this in mind when you select your spot. Don't worry if you don't have all these conditions in one place, as long as you have a bit of sun the rest can be created or provided with a little bit of extra preparatory work. In addition, although vegetables are traditionally grown in one place in the garden, if you have several small sites with great vegetable-growing prospects it is always possible to divide your plants between them. You can even grow a wide range of vegetables in containers.

Vegetables don't have to be grown in long rows. If you need only a few plants, grow only a few. As well as being neat and decorative, these clearly defined vegetable beds are easy to look after.

They might not always look perfect, but nothing beats the taste of home-grown carrots – delicious. If you pull a few that seem rather small, you can always eat them raw in a salad and leave the others in the ground to grow a little bigger.

Sun Most vegetables need plenty of light and warmth. Although some leafy varieties, such as lettuce and rocket, may cope in a little shade, if you haven't got sun, the choice of what you can grow will be limited.

Soil Soil that is full of nutrients is a must because vegetable plants are fast-growers and are always hungry. Ideally, the soil shouldn't be too stony (root veg in particular protest at stones, forking and becoming tough and inedible) and should be easy to work (or dig). *See also* page 27 for information on soil types.

Water Vegetables need regular and sufficient supplies of water. If your plants suffer water gluts or shortages, your crop will be nowhere near as abundant or as tender or tasty as it could be. Hedges and trees are notorious water-thieves, and walls may cause a rain shadow, which means that plants on the lee side don't receive any water when it rains. (This is something to bear in mind when selecting your site for growing vegetables.) Of course, you can still plant in these drier places, but you will have to be prepared to provide a good proportion of the water under your own steam. Invest in water butts, and also mulch the soil to retain moisture in these areas.

Frost pockets

While the term 'frost pocket' might sound quite attractive, your vegetables will not like to be in one. On a frosty day, take a look around your garden as the sun warms it up. You can easily spot the frost pockets – they are the places where the ground stays white and frozen longer than anywhere else.

Just as hot air rises, so cold air sinks. Low areas get much colder than higher areas, and low areas hemmed in by hedges or buildings will be even worse, as the cold air cannot escape. On a slope, making a gap in a hedge or fence can help alleviate the problem. Even after the likelihood of frost is passed in late spring, don't forget that these areas are still probably the coldest in the garden. If part of your vegetable bed is in a frost pocket, remember that hardy veg like broad beans and brassicas will cope in these colder areas, while potatoes or runner beans won't fare so well.

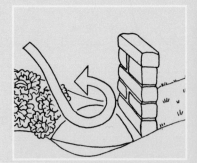

Cold air collects at the bottom of slopes or where a wall or other obstruction slows its passage. Avoid growing the more tender vegetables in such sites.

Overwintering vegetables, such as leeks and Brussels sprouts, can cope with a fair amount of frost without being killed or even spoiled.

Low box hedges and neatly trimmed box balls provide permanent structure in this vegetable garden. They also provide excellent shelter for the crops, but do bear in mind that hedges make their own demands: their roots will grow into the vegetables' space, taking nutrients and water from the soil.

Drainage Roots need air as well as water. If the soil is waterlogged (*see* box) the roots will suffocate, which means the plant they are supporting will not be able to grow. Choose a well-drained site for your vegetables or improve the drainage; this can be done by incorporating plenty of manure or compost (*see also* page 28) or by making raised beds (*see also* pages 18–20). At the other end of the scale, very free-draining soil can be equally bad – when the water runs away too quickly, the roots don't get a chance to drink. Surprisingly, the solution for very

free-draining soil is the same as for poor drainage: add some organic matter.

Exposure The perfect vegetable bed is one that is sheltered from strong, cold winds which will batter and bruise your precious crops. However, it also needs a reasonable breath of air through it to ensure pollination of certain plants, and to make it less inviting to pests and diseases. You can make an exposed site more comfortable for your vegetables by erecting a simple fence or planting a low hedge at a sensible distance.

Waterlogged soil

If you suspect your soil is poorly drained, have a closer look: mosses and rush-type plants growing in it are a giveaway, as are puddles forming and hanging about after rain. Dig a hole between 30 and 60cm (12 and 24in) deep and pour in a bucket of water; the water should drain away reasonably quickly. If the water is still there an hour or more later, you have a problem with drainage. Take heart, though, it could be that there is simply a 'pan' below the surface. This occurs when soil has been compacted by frequent walking on it, or through regular digging to the same depth.

THE SOLUTION
Make the hole a little deeper and check the consistency of the soil as you go. If you come across an area that is difficult to dig and very compacted, dig through it and try the bucket of water trick again. If it drains away more quickly this time, digging deep and adding composted material is the answer (*see also* pages 34–5). Otherwise, raised beds (*see also* page 18) are your best option – especially for those who want to grow veg in a spot where there is a high water table.

Layout

The easiest way to grow vegetables is to plant them in a traditional layout: that is in straight rows in straight-sided, not-too-wide beds with paths in between. There are many good reasons for this. Veg are plants that need lots of attention – in the form of weeding, feeding, tying up, and harvesting. If they are planted all higgledy piggledy about the place, tending them can get tiresome. Then there are the gaps that appear as you harvest the crops – these are easier to fill if they are a regular shape, plus new seedlings coming up won't get hoed along with the weeds by mistake. Narrow beds will help you to reach the plants and avoid the temptation of stepping on the soil, which will only compact it and spoil all your earlier hard digging work (*see also* page 34). However, if you really want a layout that is both pretty and practical, a potager could be the answer (*see* box, page 15).

The layout shown and described here is the ideal for vegetables. Adapt it to suit your needs and the size and shape of your plot.

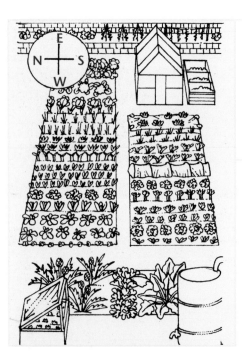

There is a good reason for every aspect of a traditional vegetable garden, from the direction the rows run – north/south to get the most sun for shorter veg plants growing behind tall ones, to the position of the greenhouse and compost heaps – easy to access but not in the way.

Careful thought has gone into the design of this plot. The wooden structures provide shelter for the vegetables and support for fruit trees; they also ensure that the vegetable garden looks interesting, even during the winter months.

You will need:

■ **Three or four main beds** – Make your main beds any length you like; the optimum width is about 1.2m (4ft), as this allows you to reach the middle without treading on the soil. Three is the perfect number as it enables straightforward rotation of crops (*see also* page 23). Run paths between the beds for easy access all around the plot.

■ **One permanent bed** – This is for perennial crops, such as asparagus and globe artichokes, which stay in place year after year.

■ **Compost bins** – Site bins within easy reach of the veg beds to make them easy to fill, turn over, and empty. Have three separate bins on the go to keep the compost-making process simple (*see also* page 30).

■ **Cold frames and/or cloches** – These are useful for raising and hardening off young plants before they are planted out into permanent beds. Cold frames are usually 1.2m x 60cm (4ft x 2ft) and made of aluminium with glass or plastic panes. Their permanent site should be reasonably bright and sheltered. Cloches are the portable version and can be moved around the vegetable patch to offer protection for rows of young plants as required.

■ **Greenhouse** – Although a greenhouse is not essential, the more you get bitten by the veg-growing bug, the more you will want one, and once you have one, you will fill it…easily. Get one as big as you can afford (larger ones retain heat longer and are easier to work in) and position it so its longer edges run north to south to make the most use of summer light. Position it out of the full blast of the wind, as this will cool it very quickly.

■ **Water** – Where you have a sloping greenhouse roof you can install a drainpipe and waterbutt, or two, to collect rainwater as it runs off. Put them by sheds and garages, too, or anywhere that water can be collected and put to good use. You will also almost inevitably need an outside tap, in a convenient position for filling watering cans or using the hosepipe.

Herbs

No vegetable garden is complete without a selection of herbs, and the majority of these do very well in containers. Some are short-lived and need to be sown regularly or bought as small plants (very cheaply) from a garden centre or supermarket. These include basil, parsley and coriander. Others will survive for a long time in a pot, needing only an annual pruning or tidy up. Mint, marjoram, chives, bay, sage and thyme fit into this category.

If you buy potted supermarket herbs, don't forget to harden them off slowly before putting them outside (*see* page 38) – they will be very delicate to begin with.

It is a common misconception that all herbs need a hot sunny position

(*see* page 38)

Potagers

Vegetables lend themselves very well to a formal layout, but that doesn't mean your creative side has to be suppressed. Potagers are vegetable gardens that have been planted to make the most of the decorative qualities of the plants, such as blocks of purple-leaved cabbages punctuated with wigwams of red-flowered runner beans, and swirls of lettuces with different foliage textures and colours surrounding a square of onions or sweetcorn. You can add flowering plants too: it is best to stick to annuals – companion plants such as marigolds are good choices – as you will probably want to dig the whole plot over, flowers and all, at the end of the season. Although the design of your potager can be as complex as you like, don't lose sight of the fact that you will need space to weed and harvest the vegetables, and that some won't appreciate being shaded out by taller neighbours.

on poor dry soil. Though most do, there are exceptions: parsley prefers cool light shade, mint needs plenty of moisture, and chives like rich soil. Their individual requirements can be met easily by growing them in pots.

Parsley is among many herbs that do well in a container. It will also tolerate some shade.

Somewhere to put your prunings, weeds and dead plants is essential in a vegetable plot. A compost bin is also a means of recycling the goodness contained within spent plant material.

From dreams to reality

If you already have a nice rectangular or square plot, neatly dug and laid with paths, and it is early spring, it's very easy to get down to the nitty gritty of growing veg; but if you're thinking 'what do I do next?', read on.

Developing a plan

Begin by listing the vegetables you would like to grow in the plot. Base this list on what you and your family enjoy eating a lot of, and not what you cook only from time to time – it's no good growing acres of beetroot if no one likes it! Also decide whether you really need to grow the types of vegetable that are cheap to buy (such as maincrop potatoes) and remember to include those that are tricky to get hold of (such as Swiss chard). If you need inspiration, have a look at the A–Z of Vegetables, *see* page 60.

Now you have some idea of the scale of your ambitions, the next step is to go out and measure up the area of your proposed vegetable garden, and then draw a sketch of the site to some sort of scale. This isn't Chelsea, no one is judging you and you don't have to be a dab hand with the crayons, simply draw a few straight lines on a piece of paper.

One of the first steps in creating a vegetable garden from scratch is to measure out the area you propose to use, then make a rough sketch of it to get an idea of the space you have available for growing crops.

Once you have planned the layout of your vegetable garden, mark it out using sand and canes, or a hosepipe will do.

Graph paper or paper with squares on it makes the task a bit simpler.

On your piece of paper, proceed as follows:

■ Mark the perimeter of the vegetable garden.
■ Sketch the three or four main beds (or the sites for raised beds) and the paths in between. Don't forget, keep the beds small to begin with, you can always increase their size later.
■ Sketch in the permanent bed for perennial veg, if you want one (*see* page 14).

■ Choose a position for the compost bins. Have these in one place if possible, you'll learn why later (*see* pages 30–1).
■ Mark in the greenhouse. Even if you can't afford to have one just yet, earmark a space for it for future reference – you can always use the area as a nursery seedbed or for raising your seedlings in cold frames until then (*see* pages 38–41).

Draw as many sketches as you like, it is easier to alter these now than the vegetable plot later. When you are

happy with what you have drawn on paper, mark out the real plot with canes or planks (for straight lines) or a hose pipe or sand (if you are going for curves). Depending on its size and shape, you could define the plot's borders first and then mark out the beds and paths. If it is going onto already prepared, weed-free soil, then half the battle is won; if not, then you need to do some work. Removing grass and weeds takes time and effort – you will get tired, but if you do a good job, you will never regret it (*see* pages 32–3).

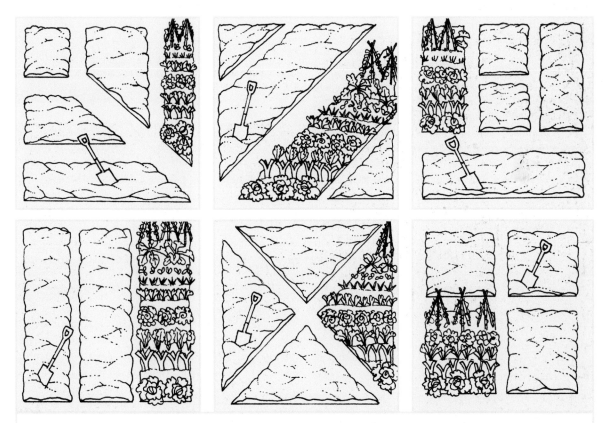

There are many ways to fit a series of vegetable beds into an area. These plans are intended to give you some ideas, but you're bound to come up with more. Remember to allow for access by making paths that are wide enough to push a wheelbarrow along them.

Growing systems versus digging

Years ago, no one would have considered growing vegetables without spending hours double digging the plot (*see* double digging, page 35). Most of us still automatically think that a vegetable garden means digging, and lots of it. However, there is a growing feeling among some veg enthusiasts that cultivation of the soil can break up its natural structure, destroying or damaging both the harmless and the helpful soil organisms and creating the kind of conditions that weeds love. It is true – tradition is not always right and ideas do change. So what are the advantages and disadvantages of each approach?

The benefits

Digging allows you to assess the texture and condition of your soil. You can use it as an opportunity to remove large stones, perennial weed roots and rubbish, to break up hard clods of earth and pans (*see* waterlogged soil box, page 13) and to incorporate organic matter (*see* page 28). After the main preparation work is done in autumn/winter, a quick fork over the soil surface once or twice in early spring, before you

There is something wonderfully satisfying about digging over your plot, breaking up hard clumps of earth and removing weeds and old vegetation. This work is done in the autumn and winter – and doing it will keep you warm!

plant your first vegetables, will bring more weed seeds up and you can hoe off any that germinate. This attention to detail will enable you to start with a reasonably weed-free patch. Make no mistake, weeds are unwanted intruders.

No-dig systems

No-dig systems rely on simply building up a layer of growing material above the soil surface; this is generally organic matter with added natural fertilizers, into which the vegetables are planted. The

benefits of this method are the comparative ease of preparation and that the valuable nutrients and soil organisms are not destroyed or disturbed. In addition, weed seeds are not disturbed and therefore, if they haven't already, they are less likely to germinate.

Deep beds and raised beds

Deep beds are for the real diggers among us – they are created by a version of double digging (*see* page 35). However, it's claimed that they have the advantage of yielding more crops per square foot of ground than conventionally cultivated plots. Experiment if you wish!

Dig down to two spades' depth, loosening the soil and working in large quantities of well-rotted organic matter as you go. Make the

Digging over a vegetable plot gives you a chance to make adjustments to the soil in order to improve its health and growing abilities. Here, horticultural sand is being added to heavy soil to improve drainage and aeration.

A raised bed provides these lettuces with optimum nutrition (plenty of organic matter has been added) and discourages some pests.

beds narrow so you can work from both sides without needing to step on the soil. If you need to fork the beds over between crops, do it from the paths alongside, or put down a temporary plank to spread your weight and avoid squashing down the soil in the bed with your feet.

This might start to sound a bit complicated, but an easier way to make a deep bed is to make a raised, or semi-raised, bed. Think of it this way: you dig to one spade's depth in your soil and then put a raised bed of one spade's depth over the area – two spade's depths, half the work. Raised beds are also a form of no-digging, in that you create your growing area above the soil surface, but many advocates break up the soil surface anyway to assist drainage, before filling the beds with soil and organic matter in which to grow their plants.

Don't forget

What about those of us who don't like digging at all, or even those of us who have no soil to dig in but still want to grow some vegetables? Well, it's good news. Vegetables are like the hare in the story about the tortoise and the hare. They grow away very quickly, using up all their energy as they go. They don't put down an extensive root run for the future, and they collapse exhausted at the end of the season, having given their all. So, despite frantic activity above ground, they need little space for their roots, and canny vegetable growers profit from this exuberance: even those gardeners who have plenty of space in their veg beds have reason to plant up some in pots. It could be that the sunniest wall for ripening tomatoes and aubergines is beside the patio, or that the lettuces always become slug fodder unless they are raised above ground level, or that the soil in the vegetable garden is infected with clubroot (see page 74). Even if you have very limited room – or no garden at all – pots will enable you to grow some of your favourite greens. And, of course, pots are essential if you want to grow your culinary herbs on the kitchen windowsill.

Although these little hurdle beds won't last as long as raised beds made from planks, they are more ornamental so are a good solution for making raised beds where your vegetable garden is in full view. Fixing the hurdles to wooden-sided beds will prolong their life.

HOW TO make a raised bed

This raised bed uses planks joined at the corners and held in place with posts, either set in concrete or hammered into the soil. You can also use railway sleepers and do away with planks and posts altogether. Although railway sleepers are pricey and heavy to manoeuvre into place, they last for years, need little or no other fixing, are great to sit on, and generally do the job just fine.

YOU WILL NEED:

- Planks – 15 x 5cm (6 x 2in) multiplied by the bed's length
- Posts – 7.5 x 7.5cm (3 x 3in) multiplied by the bed's height plus 10cm (4in) or so to fix them into the concrete
- Screws (nails may be quicker, but they are less secure)
- Hardcore or gravel – a bag or two should do
- Ready-mixed concrete
- Tools, including a drill, a spirit level and a carpenter's square

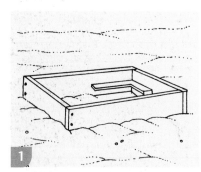

1 Decide where to put your bed; the ground needs to be reasonably level. Position and then screw the planks together for the first layer, butt-joint the timbers at the corners and use the builder's square to make sure these corner joints are straight.

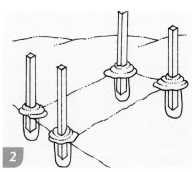

2 Dig four holes for the corner posts, using the first layer of planks as a guide for their positions. Add a handful of gravel to each post hole to allow any water to drain away. If your raised bed is very long, you may need to add some extra posts along the sides for strength.

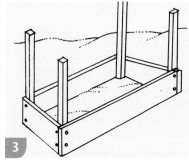

3 Set the posts into the holes on top of the gravel, check they are straight using the spirit level and add the mixed concrete. While the concrete is setting around the posts, position the first layer of planks in place. Make sure they fit snugly and are straight and level.

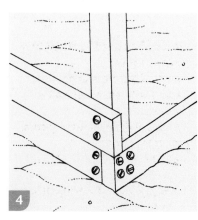

4 Once the concrete is set, build up the rest of the raised bed with planks, layer by layer, until you reach the height you require. Stagger the joints at the corners and screw the planks to each other and to the corner posts as you go.

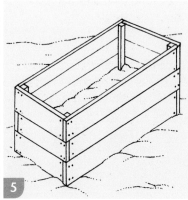

5 When construction is complete, loosen the surface of the soil inside the bed using a fork, then add a layer of gravel or hardcore a couple of centimetres (1in) deep. This is optional, but sensible if you have poorly drained or heavy soil beneath.

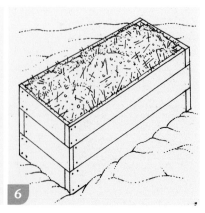

6 Fill the bed with a mixture that is half topsoil and half humus-rich material, to get your vegetable off to a good start. Overfill the bed to allow for settling.

Deciding what to grow

One of the easiest times to get carried away is when you sit down with vegetable seed catalogues or take a trip to the local garden centre and wander around all those consoles filled with tempting seed packets. Unplanned buying is a well-known phenomenon among gardeners of all ages and stages – and whatever you might think now, you will fall victim. However, you can limit the distance you fall by making as many of the decisions about what seeds to buy before you ever open a catalogue, browse the internet, or leave the house.

Well, you'll be smiling when, after a few weeks, you go out to the veg plot and return with the makings of a home-grown meal in your trug!

Top of the list
Everyone has different likes and dislikes, so tailor your choice of veg to suit your taste. These lists are intended to give you some inspiration; when you have a shortlist of candidates, read more about your choices in the A–Z of Vegetables, which starts on page 60. It gives details of the varieties of each vegetable and how to grow them – be prepared to rework your list a few times over.

Favourites
Chillies
French beans
Mangetout and sugar snap peas
New potatoes
Radishes
Runner beans
Sweetcorn
Tomatoes

Easy
Courgettes
Garlic
Onions and shallots
Rocket
Salad leaves in variety, but not necessarily lettuce
Spinach

Pricey in the shops
Asparagus (perennial)
Sprouting broccoli

Unusual and difficult to buy in the shops
Carrots of the not-orange kind
Globe artichokes (perennial)
Kohl rabi
Potatoes of the heirloom varieties, such as Pink Fir Apple
Swiss chard

To enjoy young and tender
Beetroot
Carrots
Courgettes and summer squashes
Leeks
Parsnips
Turnips

Swiss chard is hardly ever available in the shops. It is best picked and cooked straight away as it wilts soon after picking and the large leaves are easily damaged.

To inspire the kids

Children are often very keen to get involved in gardening and, of course, parents are keen to encourage them. Don't forget, though, that even one week of waiting for something to happen seems like forever to a child, so grow vegetables that are quick to mature. Help children to choose types of vegetables that they like to eat and give them the best possible spot to grow them or they'll soon become discouraged. Tomatoes, salad leaves, and baby vegetables are a good start.

More difficult to grow

Calabrese
Cauliflowers in interesting colours
Celery
Cucumber
Florence fennel

Herbs for flavour

The following need virtually no care and are generally bought as small plants:
Chives
Fennel
Marjoram
Mint
Rosemary
Sage
Thyme

To add variety

Aubergines
Brussels sprouts
Celeriac
Endive or chicory
Kale
Land cress
Peppers

With just a few herb plants you can flavour your cooking for most of the year, so you don't need much space to get a worthwhile crop. They are easy to look after, and when planted in a herb wheel like this they also make an attractive feature. Just make sure that herbs you grow together have the same growing requirements.

To grow as mini veg

Here is a selection of currently available baby vegetables, but new ones are constantly coming on the market:
Beetroot 'Pablo'
Cabbages 'Redcap', 'Shelta'
Calabrese 'Kabuki'
Courgette 'Supremo'
French beans 'Ferrari', 'Stanley'
Leek 'King Richard'
Parsnips 'Dagger', 'Lancer'
Squash 'Sunburst'
Sweetcorn 'Minipop', 'Minor'
Turnips 'Primera', 'Tokyo Cross'

Salad leaves

If your lettuces never get beyond providing local slugs and snails with tasty food on which to produce yet more offspring, try something else. Nowadays, the variety of other plant leaves that can be sown as salad crops is astonishing:

Baby spinach	Oriental leaves
Beetroot leaves	Purslane
Dandelions	Rocket
Endive	Sorrel
Lamb's lettuce	Sprouting seeds
Land cress	Watercress
Mixed salad leaves	

Because they grow quickly and are soon harvested, it is quite possible to grow salad leaves in a container or hanging basket – where they can be within easy reach of the kitchen.

Crop rotation

Unlike 'harvest' and 'dig', which everyone understands, the term 'crop rotation' seems to cause quite a bit of confusion. It needn't. Crop rotation, while very important, is not nearly as complicated as some might think. The very simple idea behind it is that you don't plant the same crop in the same bit of ground more than one year in three (or four).

Crop rotation is good for vegetable production in two main ways.

First, it is a great natural method of preventing diseases taking hold – think of it as a kind of quarantine, if you like. For example, members of the cabbage family (brassicas) can suffer from root diseases. If you continuously plant cabbages, broccoli, sprouts, and so on in the same spot, you are continuously feeding these root diseases. If you move your brassicas each year, the root diseases will 'starve'.

Second, it makes the maximum use of soil nutrients and other resources, such as manure, which are needed in varying amounts by different crops.

For example, peas and beans love a bit of muck, but carrots and parsnips don't and are happier in a bed that has been manured one or two years before.

How to rotate

The traditional way to rotate crops was to divide the plot into four equal parts, growing potatoes in one quarter, other root veg in another, peas and beans in the next, and brassicas in the last. (With salads and other quick crops planted in the gaps between rows of bigger, slower crops.) However, this traditional system doesn't take into account 'modern' crops, such as sweetcorn and courgettes, and the fact

that many people don't think it is necessary to grow maincrop potatoes. But the general principles are still sound; simply divide the plot into three and grow these newcomers with the peas and beans, or tuck them in around the other beds. An example of how this would work in practice is shown in the diagram below, with the various categories of vegetables moving from top to bottom.

If you grow your vegetables in small beds where it's not practical to follow a strict rotation, try to avoid growing the same crop on the same patch of ground every year (or two, if possible) to keep the beds in good health.

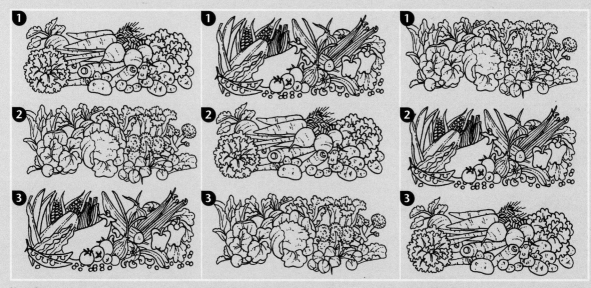

Year One
Grow roots in bed 1, brassicas in bed 2 and other vegetables in bed 3.

Year Two
Grow other veg in bed 1, roots in bed 2 and brassicas in bed 3.

Year Three
Grow brassicas in bed 1, other veg in bed 2 and roots in bed 3.

Planting and growing

Now you know what you are aiming for, it's time to get down to the nitty gritty of vegetable gardening – the ground preparation and the planting and aftercare of your vegetables. Although it can be tempting to rush the preparation in order to get to the fun bit, time spent in the beginning will repay you – and you may even find that you enjoy it.

Tools and equipment

If you have any sort of garden, you have probably already accumulated some tools; if they do the job and are pleasing to use, look no further. If you need any new implements, perhaps for digging a vegetable garden from scratch, go to your nearest garden centre or DIY store and have a look at what's on offer. Weigh up price with quality. There is rarely any need to spend a fortune, as a spade will be doing a job of work, not looking pretty in the shed.

When it comes to buying tools, it's all too easy to get carried away. Bear in mind that any tool you have in your shed will only be useful if it is used.

Digging

For digging the soil, you need a spade and a fork. Generally, forks are more versatile. Spades are good for digging lighter soils, but on heavy or stony soil, forks are less likely to get stuck, and they are excellent at ferreting about under the soil surface, loosening clumps and destroying pans of compacted soil (*see* page 13).

Forks and spades come in a variety of sizes and weights, and have either a T-handle or a D-handle – choose what is more comfortable for you. Wooden shafts have a degree of 'give' that metal does not – a relief if you are constantly digging into stony ground.

A Dutch or push hoe is one of the vegetable gardener's most hardworking tools. Through the growing season it could be in almost daily use, so make sure you choose one that you find comfortable, and sharpen its blade regularly.

Weeding

Hoes are the traditional tool of choice for weeding vegetable beds. The draw, or chop, hoe has its blade at a right angle to a longish shaft. As the name implies, it is used to chop down weeds, which it does very well. It isn't a precision instrument, so be careful around rows of delicate young seedlings. For these areas, use an onion hoe, which has a short handle and finer blade. Get down onto your knees to use it and ease it carefully around your plants. A push, or Dutch, hoe has a slightly angled blade at the end of a long shaft. The blade is pushed just under the soil surface, slicing through weeds as it goes. All hoe blades need to be sharp, otherwise they uproot rather than decapitate. Uprooted weeds are not dead: they are only too pleased to re-root, given the opportunity.

Raking

The only rake you need for veg is the type with short parallel teeth. This is used to level the soil surface in preparation for planting (*see* page 36). Don't pick an ultra-light one, as it will bounce over the soil surface, making you do all the work.

Hand tools

The most useful hand tool is a trowel, which you use for planting and surreptitious weeding. Choose one with a decently shaped blade (nice and long) that has good sharp edges. A hand fork comes in second place, but is good for planting, removing stubborn perennial weeds and a bit of spot hoeing. For removing more stubborn, deep-rooted weeds a daisy grubber may be useful. There are any number of cheap and nasty hand tools on the market. They make gardening a chore and soon break – if you ask for a set as a gift, make sure you specify the make.

Garden knives, secateurs, and a pair of well-fitting gloves all come in handy, too.

Other important items

For watering and administering liquid feed, you will need a watering can. If you plan to use weedkiller, have a plastic watering can labelled specifically for the purpose. Waterbutts are useful, even in a small garden, and hosepipes are invaluable in a larger one. An outdoor tap is almost indispensable.

Most likely you will need a wheelbarrow. Get one with pneumatic tyres as they run more smoothly. Make sure the space between the handles is wide enough for your hips and hands – they often seem to be made for stick-thin people. If your plot is very small, a flexible plastic tub-trug will do an adequate haulage job, but it does make life tough on your back.

Seed bed preparation is best done with a parallel-toothed rake. This is satisfying work, and when well done provides the perfect nursery for your young vegetables. Don't over-rake or the surface will become 'caked' when it rains.

After a while you will get to know the tools that you find most useful. Forks, spades and trowels are likely to be high on the list.

Rotavators

While they do have their place, particularly on larger plots, rotavators are not all good news, and they may not cultivate deeply enough. On the upside, they will slice up annual weeds, on the downside, they chop through the roots of perennial weeds, effectively propagating them and encouraging new growth (*see* page 32). If you must use one, hire rather than buy, just to be sure it helps, and that you can handle it.

All about soil

Despite outward appearances, soil is an immensely complex and dynamic material, full of living organisms, chemicals, minerals, and decaying matter. As a vegetable gardener you are interested in the topsoil and, to a lesser extent, the subsoil. Depending on where you live, these are made up of varying amounts of loam, sand, chalk (limestone), clay and/or peat. To get the best from your soil, it is good to know a bit about its make-up (*see* box).

Soil types – benefits and disadvantages

If you have loam, you are lucky. Loamy soil is well drained but moisture retentive, and it is naturally fertile. It is easy to dig, it is not easily compacted, and it warms up quickly in the spring, enabling you to get off to an early start with your planting. In short, gardeners and most plants love loam.

Sandy soil is often described as light soil. It is made up of large particles, with lots of air spaces, and it feels rough to the touch; water drains out of it very quickly, washing nutrients with it as it goes. Like loam, though, it is easy to dig and warms up quickly.

Chalk soils are made up of fine particles and are reasonably fertile and well drained. Chalk soil is also shallow, which means you might also get to know your subsoil quite well (*see* digging, page 34). There

Know your soil

If you are unsure of your soil type, the easiest way to assess it is to go out into the garden and have a feel. The texture of soil reveals a lot about its make-up. The soils shown here are the five basic types, but it is possible to have something that consists of a mixture of them, or even to have different soil types in different parts of your garden.

① Sandy soil is light: very loose, dry and gritty. If you grab a handful of it, it tends to flow out through your fingers.

② Clay soil is heavy: it is sticky and nearly always feels damp, except during drought when it becomes as hard as iron.

③ Chalk soil tends to be pale and lumpy. The lumps are pieces of chalk. Chalk soil dries out quickly and doesn't clump together.

④ Loam is dark brown and just looks good. It is soft in texture and when it is moist it can be squeezed into a handful but crumbles up again easily, without being sticky.

⑤ Peat is even darker than loam, and it holds water very well. If you grab a handful after rain, you can squeeze water out of it like a sponge.

are various terms used to describe chalk soil, including limey, calcium (calcified), or simply alkaline.

The particles that make up clay are very fine, so the soil has few air spaces. It tends to retain moisture and nutrients, but during dry weather it bakes hard. If you have clay soil, you are likely to dig up clumps of gooey stuff that could be used to create something on a potter's wheel. Peaty soil tends to go

with moorland environments and is naturally low in nutrients. It absorbs moisture, but also drains quickly and can be made more fertile with relative ease.

Alkaline or acid?

Like everything else in life, soil has a chemical balance that makes it anything from very alkaline to very acid. The scale used to measure soil acidity or alkalinity is called pH –

and it varies from pH 1 (very acid) through pH 7 (neutral) to pH 14 (very alkaline). Luckily, the extremes (1 and 14) are rare. The chemical balance of the soil can make certain nutrients unavailable to plants, so it has an impact on how well they grow. Most vegetables will produce their highest yields on neutral soil, although members of the cabbage family (brassicas) prefer growing in slightly alkaline soil for best results.

The most effective way to find out the pH of your soil is to buy a testing kit from the garden centre; these are cheap, easy to use and accurate enough for our purposes. You can also make some deductions as follows: chalky soil is alkaline, peaty soil is acid. With plants that prefer acid soil, the leaves tend to go yellow when they are grown on neutral or alkaline soils (because they can't get the iron they need).

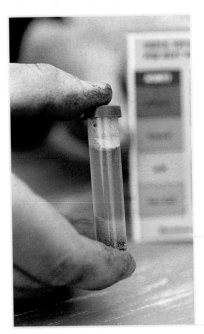

Altering the pH

While you can slightly influence the pH of your soil, drastic alterations are not only expensive, they are also only a temporary fix and so are not recommended. A garden that has been well tended over many years with the addition of plenty of compost and manure, will have become slightly more acid; the traditional 'remedy' for this is to add lime. This can be normal lime, Dolomitic lime, which contains more nutrients, particularly magnesium, or calcified seaweed – which has all the trace elements in it as well.

Adding lime

If your soil is slightly acidic and you want to add lime to make it more neutral, do this in the early autumn, well before the time in late autumn that you want to dig in your compost or manure. You need to allow a few weeks for the lime to slowly leach into the soil, otherwise it will scorch your plants and may not have time to alter the pH. Adding lime at the rate of about 500g per sq metre (1lb per sq yard) will alter the pH by one point, depending on the variety of lime you choose (the container it comes in will tell you how much to use for the area you wish to treat). Personally, I'd only add lime on a regular basis to acid soil where I wanted to grow brassicas; it also discourages clubroot (*see* page 74).

Testing kits to find out the pH of your soil are widely available at garden centres and are simple and fun to use. Follow the instructions carefully, otherwise you may get a false reading. This result indicates that the soil is neutral to slightly acid.

Improving your soil

Although tinkering with pH levels helps to increase fertility by releasing nutrients, the addition of organic matter is by far the most important way of improving your soil structure and nutrient content, followed very closely, especially for veg, by using a fertilizer to increase productivity.

Organic matter

After clearing the site, the first step in preparing your patch is to dig in organic matter. Also known as humus, organic matter is anything that was once a growing plant and is now decaying. It comes from the compost that you make from your garden and kitchen waste and the manure produced by herbivorous animals. When it is ready to put on the garden, it is soft with a flaky or crumbly texture. Even if it once came out of a cow or horse, it doesn't smell unpleasant (if it does, it isn't rotted enough). It has umpteen benefits:

■ It acts like a sponge, holding onto moisture so the ground doesn't dry out too fast, especially in dry, hot summers and periods of drought.
■ It creates lots of tiny air spaces that allow excess rainwater to drain away faster, thereby preventing the soil from becoming waterlogged.
■ It makes the soil 'softer' and 'looser' so that roots are able to spread through it more easily.
■ It contains flourishing colonies of beneficial soil bacteria that break the material down to humus and release valuable trace elements – often severely lacking in ground that's been cultivated over some time using only fertilizers.

You know you are a real gardener when you start to look forward to adding manure to the soil. When well rotted, this material is truly a gardener's gold.

The nutrients

The three most important plant nutrients are nitrogen (N), phosphates (P), and potassium (or potash, K). There are also plenty of other trace elements that a plant finds useful. The packet in which you purchase any fertilizer will show the proportions of NPK it contains, as well as any trace elements (or micronutrients), such as boron (B), copper (Cu), iron (Fe), manganese (Mn), chlorine (Cl), and zinc (Zn). Don't worry, all you really need to know is the proportions of NPK in a fertilizer and what these do for your plants.

Feeding the soil

Vegetables are raised intensively and, although it is wonderful, organic matter doesn't provide enough of the main nutrients to keep hardworking, heavy-cropping plants supplied, so you need to use fertilizer as well. There are two types of fertilizer, those that you add during soil preparation, which are covered here, and those that you give as regular feeds during the growing season, which are described on page 47. Soil-preparation fertilizers are in the form of pellets, powders and granules; these break down slowly in the soil hanging about so the growing plants can make use of them as needed. Using fertilizer doesn't mean you have to throw your 'organic' principles out of the window, as there are plenty of organic fertilizers on the market derived from natural sources.

General-purpose fertilizers

These offer a balanced feed, containing roughly equal quantities of NPK (*see* box). Use them to ensure that your crops get a bit of everything they need. Sprinkle it evenly over the soil and lightly work it into the surface when preparing the patch in late winter or early spring, and when you've cleared a row of crops in summer and are going to replant. Perennial veg, like artichokes and asparagus, appreciate it at the start of the growing season (mid- to late spring), too. Follow the instructions on the packet, but as a rough guide use about a handful per square metre.

Nitrogen-rich fertilizers

Designed to help the plant in its leaf production, they include chicken manure pellets, hoof and horn, and seaweed meal. Apply chicken manure

Before sowing another crop where one has just been cleared, always give the ground a sprinkling of general-purpose fertilizer and rake it in to feed the soil.

pellets before sowing or planting green veg. Hoof and horn is slow-acting and organic; it is best applied very early in spring. Seaweed meal, which should appeal to vegetarians, is also rich in potassium and is a renewable resource; rake it in before planting in spring.

Phosphate-rich fertilizers

Beneficial for establishing strong root systems. Although bonemeal contains plenty of phosphates, it tends not to be available to the plants; blood, fish and bone provides a better source of food.

High-potash feed

This is given to produce flowers and fruit. It is usually sold as sulphate of potash, which is appreciated by heavy-cropping, fruiting plants, such as tomatoes. Organic high-potash feeds are also available.

Organic or not?

Nowadays, gardeners are much better educated about the pros and cons of using chemical and other means to enrich the soil. 'Natural' fertilizers do a good job and feed soil micro-organisms too, but it can be tempting to use chemicals because they are often cheaper and very quick-acting – think of it as being like an instant sugar-fix and it won't seem quite so attractive. Inorganic fertilizers also work independently without interacting with the soil, which can become lifeless in the long run. Even the faster-acting organic feeds will do more for the health of your soil than the pure chemical ones.

Perhaps we should also consider the ethics behind manufactured fertilizers. For example, the chickens that provide the chicken manure pellets might be factory farmed, and there is no putting a pleasant slant on blood, fish and bone. Manure from animals can also contain chemicals, such as antibiotics and dewormers. To my mind, if you are going to eat it, it seems best that veg is produced as wholesomely as possible.

Now you know the benefits of organic matter, you'll understand why you need a compost bin (or three). Learning how to make good compost is one of the most useful things a vegetable grower can do.

The main principle in making good compost is to use plenty of different material: mix fine waste such as grass with coarse waste such as potato peelings; use dry waste such as unprinted paper and cardboard with wet waste such as annual weeds and crop trimmings. This mixture contains a careful balance of air and moisture, providing suitable conditions for the bacteria that rot down the heap. The bacteria are responsible for creating heat as they work and this heat increases their numbers. Worms and other organisms in the mixture also help the decaying process.

There are some people who say they compost everything, right down to the kitchen sink, and it all comes out as a beautiful, rich, brown, sweet-smelling humus. Well, lucky them. In reality, almost any kitchen or garden waste can go into the bin, except

This neat compost bin, complete with hinged lid, is simple to make and will repay a few hours' work with years of service.

cooked food and meat, which may attract rats. And it goes without saying, don't put cat or dog muck into the mix as it contains harmful pathogens.

To speed up the compost-making process, make sure that everything is well mixed. I reckon life is too short to keep turning it later. If you have added woody material, you may have to return it to the heap for another session, as it is much slower to rot down.

The ideal is to have three bins: one is rotting down, one is being added to, one is ready for use; two will do, though. Top of the range are the wooden bins, which look great and do a good job. You can also use the wide-bottomed plastic bins that look a little like Daleks; drill some more holes in them for drainage, and water their contents regularly to speed things up.

Who would have thought this pretty little doll's house was a repository for all the garden's waste materials?

HOW TO make a wooden compost bin

The ideal wooden bin is 1m (3ft) square or bigger. The bin shown here is made from planks attached to posts. The planks are held in place on three sides with screws or nails, and at the front they are slid into batten guides, so you can empty the bins with ease. There is no need to secure it to the ground. This step-by-step describes one bin. If you want more, you can simply add them on at the side, using two more posts and adding three sides of planks.

YOU WILL NEED:

- Planks – 15 x 2cm (6 x ¾in) by 1–1.4m (3–4ft)
- Battens – 5cm (2in) square by 1–1.4m (3–4ft)
- Posts – 10 x 10cm (4 x 4in) by 1–1.4m (3–4ft)
- Screws or nails (nails are quicker but are less secure)
- Tools, including a drill or hammer, a spirit level and a carpenter's square

Decide where to put your bins; ideally the ground should be reasonably level. Lay two posts, cut to size, on the ground and start to attach the cut planks to them, either with screws or nails. Leave a small gap about 8–10cm (3–4in) at the bottom to ensure that the bin sits level.

Make the second side in exactly the same way as the first.

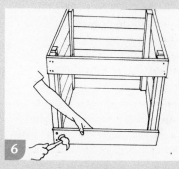

Measure and cut two battens to fit 2.5cm (1in) behind what will become the front two posts. Nail or screw them in place.

Put a small piece of wood at the bottom of each batten guide for the lowest sliding plank to rest on.

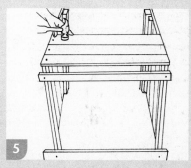

Use temporary battens to hold the two sides in place while you attach the planks. Check the corners stay square.

Cut and attach a strengthening plank to the top and bottom of the bin front.

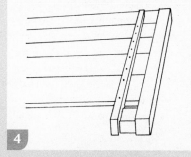

Cut and fit the sliding planks.

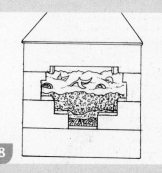

Add compost – mix the material well and dampen it down if necessary. Lay a tarpaulin over the top to retain the heat.

Preparing your plot

Now you are fully armed with all the information you need, it is time to get out there and prepare your plot. It may seem a bit boring, but the hard work that you do now will stand you in good stead for years and years to come. Do preparation work in good time for planting in spring – this means starting in autumn, if at all possible.

First time around

If you are creating a new patch, you must first remove any grass and/or weeds, and then – just as important – dig in loads of organic material.

When faced with an uncultivated piece of ground, a lot of people make the mistake of hiring a rotavator and pushing it around to chop up weeds or turf. They then bury the lot and start planting straight away. Don't do it! Strange as it sounds, rotavating propagates perennial weeds; it does this very efficiently by chopping their roots into hundreds of root cuttings, all of which turn into new plants, and

Spend some time digging out large stones and builder's rubble. This can be a hard job, but you'll regret it if you don't do it.

it does nothing to discourage the destructive soil pests that are usually prevalent in old grassland.

Grass and weeds

If your proposed vegetable garden is covered with grass, your first job is to strip off the turf. Use a spade and skim it off the ground in slices 4cm (1½in) thick so you get most of the roots,

too. Stack the pieces upside down in an out-of-the-way corner of your garden and over 18 months or so they will turn into good fibrous loam that you can recycle back onto the garden. If instead of grass you have rough or overgrown ground to contend with, dig out brambles, tree seedlings, perennial weeds and any annual weeds with seedheads; you can leave smaller, non-seeding annual weeds, as they can safely be dug back in.

Organic material

Once the majority of the weeds have been removed, dig the ground roughly, using a fork. Take out large stones, roots, and any other rubbish. Now dig it over again, this time using a spade, working in as much well-rotted organic matter as possible. A barrow-load per square metre/yard isn't too much when you're breaking in new ground; a bucketful per metre/yard is enough for ground that's previously been well cultivated but allowed to run wild for a time. If you've only just started gardening and haven't made any of your own compost, phone around local livery

Once you have marked out the site of your plot – in this case a circular herb bed – you need to remove what's there. If it's grass, begin by stripping the turf around the perimeter. This reveals the shape of your bed in the flesh and offers you a final opportunity for fine-tuning.

stables, mushroom farms, smallholders, and so on to see if they have any organic material to spare.

Relax (a bit)

Leave the ground alone for several months so that birds and other natural predators can remove soil pests and slugs or snails. It's a good idea to fork over the area occasionally to expose more pests so that predators can continue to reduce the population. This also helps to reduce your weed population, as it brings dormant weed seeds to the surface where sunlight 'triggers' them to germinate. Hoe off these new crops of weed seedlings or flame-gun them before they have time to set seed or become established. The more of this you can do before you start to cultivate a new plot, the easier it will be to manage the patch later. Also, this is the time to add lime, if necessary (*see* page 28).

Now for the fun bit

Before planting, fork over the ground, removing any last-minute weeds, sprinkle on a general-purpose fertilizer (*see* page 29) and rake it in, removing any stones and roots as you go so the ground ends up clean, level and ready to go.

Regular maintenance

The soil used for growing annual vegetables benefits from a little attention every time it falls vacant.

Weedkillers

There is a lot to be said for using weedkiller to clear a plot that is dreadfully overgrown with perennial weeds, but you need plenty of time to ensure it can do the job properly, and you must accept that this is not an organic solution.

Choose a total, non-residual weedkiller, such as glyphosate. Use it according to the manufacturer's instructions. Spray it onto weeds or use a watering can fitted with a fine rose or 'dribble bar'. Apply in late spring or early summer when the weeds will be growing strongly, and choose a still day (so you don't get uncontrolled drift onto areas of the garden that you don't want to treat).

The glyphosate is absorbed through the leaves and slowly kills the roots, so it'll be several weeks before the green tops appear to start dying off. When this happens you can clear the remains of the weeds away by hand or let them dry out before burning them off with a flame-gun. Wait four to six weeks to see if re-growth occurs. If it does, repeat the chemical spray treatment as soon as the weeds are a few centimetres high, so that there's enough foliage to absorb the product, but not so much that the weeds regain their strength. Long-established colonies of perennial weeds may need three or four treatments to completely eradicate the problem. Allow six or eight weeks after apparent death to be absolutely certain that they won't grow back before you begin cultivating the ground with vegetables and herbs.

Spent mushroom compost doesn't contain many nutrients, but it is a great soil conditioner.

Autumn

Each autumn, as soon as summer crops have been cleared, spread well-rotted organic matter on those areas that won't be used for growing root vegetables, such as parsnips, carrots or potatoes, next year. A few weeks later, hoe off or otherwise remove re-emerging weeds from the soil surface.

Winter and spring

Continue digging and adding organic matter over the winter and early spring as winter crops are harvested and cleared, so that by spring the whole plot is ready to go.

Summer

Even in summer it's worth doing a little light soil improvement every time you clear rows of salads or other short-term crops. Clear away the old roots and leaves, plus any weeds, taking care not to disturb adjacent rows of plants, then sprinkle some organic general-purpose fertilizer over the bare soil and work it lightly into the ground with a rake before sowing or planting your next crop. This replaces lost nutrients and makes sure growing conditions are back up to scratch so the whole space stays as productive as possible all season.

FOCUS ON Digging

The main purpose of digging is to break up the soil and to incorporate organic matter. Single digging (digging to the depth of a spit – the spade blade) is sufficient for most purposes, but very heavy or poor soils may require more drastic action (double digging).

HOW TO single dig

Single digging is excavating soil to a spit deep and moving it along the bed. As you move the soil it is easy to take out the roots of persistent weeds, break up large clumps of earth and remove large stones and other debris. It gives you a chance to assess the health of your soil and learn a little more about its character, such as how well drained it is, or whether there are pockets of clay or chalk that might need breaking up a bit more thoroughly.

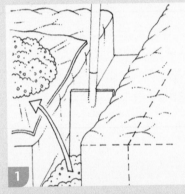

1 Dig a trench to one spit's depth and width. Place the extracted soil on thick plastic sheeting (or in a wheelbarrow). Leave it there as you will need it later. Remove any weeds as you go along.

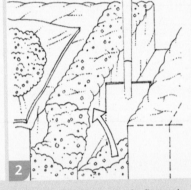

Dig another trench next to the first and put the soil from it into the first trench. Add any soil improvers if necessary. Continue in this way until you get to the final trench.

3 When you've extracted the soil from the final trench, fill it with the soil you've kept from the first trench. Go over the whole area and break up any lumps with the spade or a garden fork.

Invest in a good-quality wheelbarrow: it will make light work of transporting weighty compost around the garden.

HOW TO double dig

Double digging involves cultivating the soil to the depth of two spits. If you have a bad pan in your garden or very poor soil that is full of debris, such as builder's waste for example, you might decide to double dig – a few days later, when you are nursing your backache, you might regret your decision. But double digging has its place, and can do some good by loosening the subsoil without bringing it nearer the surface. If you do feel your plot would benefit, why not do it over a few years, focusing on one area at a time?

1

Using a spade, make a trench as for single digging. Remove the soil to a wheelbarrow (or large sheet of plastic). You will need this later.

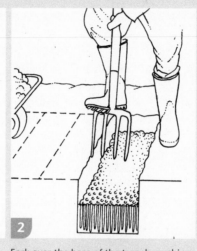

2

Fork over the base of the trench, pushing the fork tines in to their full depth to loosen and aerate compacted soil as much as possible.

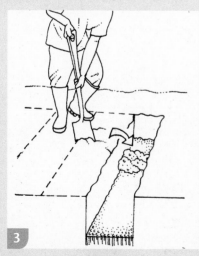

3

Now using the spade again, dig a new trench and turn this next batch of topsoil into the previous trench. Add plenty of organic matter to improve the soil quality.

4

Continue digging in this way until you reach the final trench. Having forked over the base, fill this final trench with the soil you have kept from the first.

Take care with this back-breaking work

In the 'good old days' much was made of digging: single digging, double digging, trenching, and so on. Nowadays, we tend to turn a bit of soil over and think we've worked hard. So, for those of us who are not accustomed to this kind of toil:

■ Don't be tempted to get carried away and overdo digging in your first session, especially if you are not used to such physical work. Digging exercises muscles in the shoulders, stomach and back that many of us don't know we have.

■ Keep the blade upright so that the spade achieves maximum depth with minimum effort.

■ Lift small spadefuls at a time, not mammoth ones. Remember damp soil is much heavier to lift than dry.

■ Do it little and often to protect your back from damage – no more than half an hour at a stretch.

■ Don't work when the ground is wet or frozen – you will do more harm than good. The soil is more likely to become compacted in these conditions. You can help protect the soil by standing on a scaffold plank to spread your weight.

Propagation

By far the most common way to raise vegetables is from seed, although there are important exceptions (*see* page 41). Most vegetables are sown directly into the soil where the plants will grow and mature, although, again, there are exceptions, such as plants that are tender (tomatoes and sweetcorn) and those that don't need much space at first (leeks and brassicas). Information on planting and cultivation requirements are given in the A–Z, which begins on page 60, and is also provided on most seed packets.

Direct sowing

For sowing seeds directly, prepare the soil using a rake to create a 'fine tilth' – this means that the top couple of centimetres of soil are free from stones and big clods of earth, which the tiny seedlings would otherwise have to struggle around, at best wasting valuable energy and at worst giving up before they had even really got going.

Make a straight shallow groove, called a 'drill', in the soil. You can do this by lightly dragging a bamboo cane or the corner of a hoe along the surface. If you are keen to have your drills absolutely straight, use a length of string tied to two pieces of

cane and pulled tight at each end as a guide. Don't worry, though, there won't be an inspection by the sergeant major afterwards.

Sprinkle the seeds very thinly along the drill, then cover them to roughly their own depth – don't bury them too deeply or they'll never make it to the surface. Use garden soil to cover them if it's fine and stone-free, but with heavy clay or soil that stays wet for a while after rain, use sharp sand or horticultural vermiculite as a cover. This gives seedlings better drainage and is easy for the tiny plants to push up through. Add a label to remind you what you have planted. In cold weather, consider covering the newly sown seed with horticultural fleece (*see* page 39).

Sowing small seeds thinly is a difficult art to master and inevitably you will drop big groups in some places – don't worry about it, everyone does it. Some people have 'techniques', such as mixing seeds with sand or putting them on a piece of folded paper, which they then tap to deposit the seed along

Left: Mark out each seed row using a length of string tied to two canes. Stand on the line to keep it taught and use the corner of a hoe to make a shallow groove or 'drill' in which to plant the seeds.

Fast-growing crops can be sown in among other vegetables or even in borders with ornamental plants. Rake the area over to break up the soil surface, sow your seeds and water in. A few twiggy pea sticks laid over the soil will act as a deterrent for cats and for birds intent on a dust bath.

About seeds

Most seeds are sold loose in packets and range from tiny (carrots and lettuce) to huge (broad beans and courgettes). In general, the smaller the seed the more you get in a packet, the shallower you sow it, and the more thinning you will need to do. With some big seeds, such as cucumbers, you only get six or so in the packet. This might seem odd, but it makes sense because one or two cucumber plants produce lots of cucumbers, whereas each carrot seed produces only one carrot.

Large seeds, such as beans (1), are sown individually. Tiny seeds, such as carrots (2) are scattered onto the compost or soil.

the drills. Experiment and find what works best: it's worthwhile, since you will reduce waste and work.

If you are filling gaps in your vegetable patch, or want to plant vegetables among ornamentals, you could try broadcast sowing, which results in a more casual effect. Simply sprinkle the seeds thinly over the cleared area without worrying about rows or drills, then cover them with a layer of sieved earth, sand or vermiculite. The only major disadvange of broadcast sowing is that you won't initially be able to tell seedlings from weedlings.

Thinning is important if you want to ensure a good strong crop. Place fingers on the soil on either side of the seedling to be removed to prevent others coming with it when you pull.

Thinning

When the seedlings appear, keep the soil between the rows well weeded so they aren't swamped. This is when you are glad you sowed in straight lines, as you will be able to identify the wanted from the unwanted. As soon as they are big enough to handle easily, thin out the seedlings. It might be heartbreaking, but it is necessary, otherwise you will have a poor crop of weak and unappetizing vegetables. Long ago, or more recently, someone has sat down and worked out how far apart each type of vegetable needs to be in order to grow at its best (spacings are given in the A–Z), you just have to do the dirty work. Simply go along the rows pulling out those that are badly crowded, damaged or weak. If your soil is very light, put two fingers on either side of the seedling that is to be removed to avoid disturbing its more fortunate neighbours. Alternatively, you can pinch off the top growth to kill the seedlings where they are. Do thinning in stages to ensure you keep the strongest specimens. You should end up with a row of young plants at the recommended spacing.

Sowing under cover

Sowing seed in pots in a greenhouse, cold frame or on a bright windowsill is the best way to raise frost-tender vegetables such as sweetcorn, French and runner beans, courgettes and pumpkins. These plants need a long growing season and are best sown in mid-April, however, they won't survive outside until after the last frost (usually around mid-May). The same technique is useful for producing early crops of other veg before conditions are favourable outside, and for when pigeons or mice are a problem (they'll often pinch early-sown pea or bean seeds).

Fill seed trays or small individual pots with seed compost. Sow large seeds, such as peas or sweetcorn, at the rate of one or two per pot. Cover the seed lightly with compost. Label the pots and/or trays – it's a good idea to add the date, too, for interest and future reference. When the seedlings emerge, if there are more than one per pot, remove the weakest, leaving just one. With smaller seeds, such as lettuce, sow them as thinly as you can; when the seedlings have a couple or more 'true' leaves (not the rounded 'seed' leaves) prick them out singly into small pots. Don't feel obliged to prick out every single one, just do as many as you need plus a few for spares and emergencies.

Hardening off

Plant out the young plants when the pot is full of roots or, in the case of frost-tender plants (tomatoes and courgettes), after the last frost. Harden off the seedlings carefully first. Don't be in a hurry; if necessary, put the plants into bigger pots so that they can be kept under

A cold frame is invaluable in a vegetable garden, acting as a halfway house for young seedlings before they make the transition into the wide world.

HOW TO prick out seedlings

1 When young seedlings in seed trays have two 'true' leaves, it is time to move them to larger quarters. Water the trays about an hour beforehand. Ease out the contents onto your potting bench.

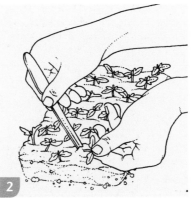

2 Using a plant label, or a dibber, carefully separate individuals from the bunch. Hold them by their seed leaves (the first leaves to emerge) and ease the roots away from their companions. Try to retain some soil around the roots of each seedling.

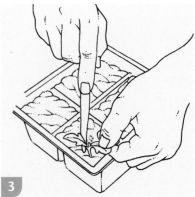

3 Plant the seedlings individually into pre-prepared pots or cells. Gently firm the soil around the roots and water in well. Put the seedlings in a partially shaded, not too hot, place for a day or so until you can be sure they have recovered from the ordeal.

plant out seedlings

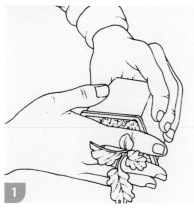

1

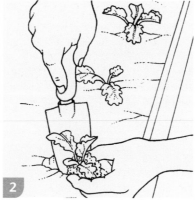

2

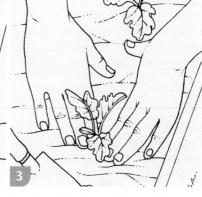

3

Once seedlings have filled the pot with roots, they can be planted out, after hardening off. Tip the pot on its side, or up-end it, and gently tip the plant out.

Make a hole big enough to take the plant's rootball without damage. If the soil around is hard, dig through it quickly to loosen it up. Plant the seedling.

Ease the soil back around the seedling's roots and firm down well, but gently. Water in the newly planted seedlings. Continue to water regularly as they grow.

cover for longer without suffering if the weather isn't welcoming.

Because frost-tender plants are raised in warm, still, humid conditions, they are rather soft and delicate and will receive a terrible shock if stuck straight outside without warning. Hardening off gives them a chance to acclimatize to outdoor conditions.

Start hardening off about two or three weeks before you want to plant out (again, the A–Z will give you information on timing). If you have a cold frame, stand the young plants in that: close the lid at night and open it every day. On cold, windy or rainy days, leave the lid closed all the time. If you don't have a cold frame, stand the plants out in the garden on fine days and bring them in at night into an unheated greenhouse or conservatory, a shed, utility room or even a cool windowsill indoors.

Planting out seedlings

Once the weather forecast, or local knowledge, suggests that all the frosts are over in your area, plant out your seedlings. Again, don't hurry, a couple of days longer in their pots will make no difference to the end result, and one frost certainly will.

Prepare the planting hole first by loosening the soil and then making an appropriate-sized hole in it. Tip the plant out of its pot carefully, without breaking up its ball of roots. Place it in the hole and refill around it, then press firmly but gently so it sits tightly and securely in the soil. Now water (*see* box, page 41). Most plants should be positioned so that the top of the rootball is slightly buried, but some, such as tomatoes and brassicas, do best if they are planted a little deeper, as it gives their stems more stability. When slightly buried the tomato stems will also take root, which makes the

Fleece is a wonderful product – protective enough to keep out the cold, but light enough not to damage the young crop. And it's relatively inexpensive too.

plants even sturdier. When your plants are finally out in the big wide world, have some horticultural fleece at the ready. This inexpensive, thin, soft, light fabric can be placed temporarily over your youngsters to give them a bit of protection if necessary.

Sowing into a seedbed

Frost-hardy crops, such as leeks and brassicas, as well as lettuce, are often raised in a seedbed outside and transplanted to their final site when they are big enough.

A very pleasing bed full of healthy young lettuces. Lettuces are often grown in a nursery bed or raised in a cold frame, ready to be planted out into the vegetable garden when space becomes available.

Frost-tender chilli plants are easily started off on a windowsill. Although this is the perfect place to germinate the seeds, it is already clear that these youngsters are leaning towards the light. To ensure even growth, turn the seed tray regularly.

Choose a sheltered corner that gets sun for at least half the day and where the young plants can be given special care. It is helpful to have a cold frame, but not essential. Prepare the ground well (as for the main vegetable bed, *see* page 36), then rake it until the surface is smooth and level – a fine tilth. Sow the seeds as in direct sowing (*see* page 36). When the seedlings appear, thin them out in stages until they are 5–7.5cm (2–3in) apart.

Transplanting seedlings

When they have 2–3 'true' leaves (the ones that recognizably belong to a leek or cabbage), dig up the seedlings with as much root as possible. Then transplant them into well-prepared soil where you want them to grow, at their final spacings. New transplants, especially lettuce, often flop when first moved, but they soon perk up.

Replant most seedlings only very slightly deeper than they were originally growing in their seedbeds, and remember to firm them in. With brassicas, plant them slightly deeper so that the first set of leaves are only just above the soil – otherwise the plants will never be strong nor heart up properly. Don't loosen up the surrounding ground too much beforehand either; brassicas need a firm hold. They should stand up straight away.

Nursery-raised plants

The business of growing and selling baby plants has burgeoned in recent years. Most garden centres and seed catalogues offer a wide range of decorative 'plug' plants, and many have a good selection of veg, too.

The 'plug' bit refers to the tiny pellets of compost that these young plants are growing in. They are fine in the rarified conditions of the nursery greenhouses, but they can suffer in the garden centre and beyond, especially from capricious watering. If you buy plug plant vegetables, even via mail order, be prepared to pot them up or harden them off and plant them out as soon as possible.

These are a good way of trying out something new or replacing something that failed, and they can be fun, but just make sure you take extra good care of them in their early days. Some garden centres also offer a limited range of vegetable plants in larger pots, which offers you the opportunity to try out several different varieties of tomato, for example, without having to buy too many packets of seed. They will also need some precautionary TLC.

Nowadays many garden centres offer a range of young vegetable plants. If you want to give in to temptation, pay a visit in spring and enjoy buying all sorts of babies, like these young sweetcorn, that are the perfect age for potting on or even planting straight out into the garden (after hardening off, of course).

Vegetables not grown from seed

There are a few vegetables that are never, or hardly ever, grown from seed by your average gardener. These include potatoes, which are grown from 'seed potatoes', maincrop onions, which are grown from 'sets', and asparagus, which are grown from 'crowns'. The A–Z gives all the specific information you will need for growing these crops.

Like nature, vegetable gardeners are always itching to fill a bare patch of soil and make the most of any available space. As a result they have developed some crafty ways of getting more out of their plot than you might have thought possible: intercropping, catch cropping, and successional sowing.

Intercropping

Intercropping is the sort of thing that you might do when you find you have a tray of young lettuce plants and nowhere obvious to put them. It's a great way to work your vegetable bed really hard, so it's particularly valuable if you don't have much space. Basically, in areas where you have slow-growing veg, you can double up on the planting by squeezing in some speed merchants.

Intercropping sounds easy, and often it is, but you do need to take into account the amount of shade any of these slow- and fast-growing partnerships are going to create – nothing will thrive too close to leafy potato plants, for example – and how will you harvest your early veg without disturbing your more sedate late veg? To make intercropping work well, you need to plan quite carefully.

One popular and attractive set of plants to grow together is courgettes, sweetcorn and runner beans. In theory, the faster-growing courgettes and runner beans grow up and through the slower-growing sweetcorn. However, in reality, if you get your spacing wrong between plants, you can find yourself crawling through a jungle of leaves and stems, looking for courgettes that are so hidden away that they have managed to grow into large marrows in the meantime. The runner beans would have liked the shade, but this dense undergrowth has invited all the slugs

This is a combination of intensive cropping and companion planting (*see* pages 52–3). Both the garlic and the carrots can be harvested at around the same time, in early to midsummer, and the garlic may deter carrot fly.

Making the most of any gaps that appear in the veg garden involves having something to go in when other veg come out. Here, leeks have been raised in a nursery bed to take the place of harvested new potatoes.

and snails in the neighbourhood to take up residence – and they love beans. You have been warned!

Catch cropping

There are two main periods in the year when large gaps appear in the vegetable garden: spring, before planting, and again in autumn, after harvesting but before you plant out overwintering crops. This is when you can do a bit of catch cropping. Like intercropping, it is a matter of planting fast-growers, but this time they're on their own. You harvest them just before your longer-term overwintering vegetables, such as cabbage, kale and garlic, go in.

Plants that are suitable as catch crops are usually the same characters as for fast-growing intercrops. Either sow them directly or (particularly in spring) raise them under cover to give them a quicker start. If you have a cloche or cold frame for protection,

you can plant them out quite early to get a crop even sooner.

Successional sowing

If you have never grown vegetables before (or even if you have) it is easy to end up with a huge amount of veg all ready to be harvested and eaten at about the same time. Successional sowing was invented to avoid this.

This is when you plant little and often – say, a short row of lettuce every two or three weeks – so you don't end up with twenty lettuces all at the peak of perfection on 16 June. Even when you know the theory, successional sowing isn't always easy to get right, due to uncontrollable influences – usually the weather. When it comes to veg growing, any planting plan has to be constantly adjusted and amended. But having a Plan B, or even C, is one of the joys of growing your own. You can make vegetable gardening as efficient and complex as you like.

Watering

Vegetables are very shallow rooted and you can't afford to let them dry out at all during their growing season. Providing water and clever ways to retain moisture is crucial in all but the wettest summers and/or wettest areas, and even then, if you have a greenhouse or grow veg in containers, watering will be a daily priority. To reduce the need for watering overall, add plenty of organic matter to the soil when you are preparing it (*see* page 28), and water in the early morning or evening to allow the plants to drink up the moisture without competition from the sun.

Supplies

Apart from falling from the sky, water is delivered to plants in two main ways – hosepipes and watering can – and from two main sources – tap and waterbutt. When you get keen on vegetable growing, you will want an outside tap, if you haven't got one already, but there is little excuse nowadays not to have a waterbutt or two as well to collect rainwater. You can connect waterbutts to any drain downpipe, including those on garages,

greenhouses and sheds (fit guttering to channel down rainwater from the roof to a waterbutt, if there isn't any already).

Hoses are excellent for watering the whole vegetable garden and can be used with a sprinkler. Hoses with holes in (seeper hoses) are better as they can be left permanently around the vegetables and so make sure the water goes where it is needed. If you are ultra-efficient, you can put a timer on the tap to water plentifully and regularly, too. However, if there

is a hosepipe ban you will have to resort to a watering can, which on the upside will bring you closer to your plants.

It is generally held that watering seedlings from waterbutts is not a good idea as the butt may harbour diseases. In practice, it depends on various factors, such as how often the water in the butt changes, but if in doubt, only use butt water on adult plants. Also, while grey water (ex-bath and washing-up water)

Is it easier in containers?

There are many advantages to growing plants in containers: you have far more influence over the soil conditions and can avoid some soil-borne diseases, it is easier to keep weeds under control and limit damage by pests such as slugs and snails, and all the food and water you provide goes directly to the plant for which it is intended. This last – water – is the chief disadvantage of growing in pots: the plants rely almost entirely on you for their water, and they need a lot of it and regularly. As far as possible use large pots, ideally between 30–40cm (12–15in), or even bigger. Smaller ones dry out too quickly once the crops get going. Terracotta pots dry out faster than glazed ones, so choose the latter if you think you might miss out on the watering from time to time.

Left: With a little thought, you can soon become a water-saving expert. Although it doesn't look all that pretty, this set-up will provide plenty of water.
Above: For the more discreet among us, a waterbutt can be disguised with screens and plants.

Vegetables, such as peas, that are sown in the ground where they are to grow have the best opportunity to find the natural supplies of water, so are less likely to suffer from a lack of water.

Greenhouse plants

Plants that are going to stay in the greenhouse their whole life are particularly vulnerable to drying out during hot weather. In greenhouse borders, bury the neck of a plastic bottle with the bottom cut off beside each plant and pour copious amounts of water into it. This way the water goes down to the roots rather than simply dampening the soil surface. If you don't have plastic bottles, sink pots into the soil – this will achieve the same result (*see* below).

If the plants are growing in pots, stand the pots on trays and fill these with water, then the plant can suck up as much as it needs over a longer period. If there is still lots of water in the tray when you check an hour or so later, tip it out so the roots don't drown.

might be fine on ornamental plants, it is not suitable for watering plants you are going to eat.

Direct-sown plants

It stands to reason that direct-sown plants and potatoes are best off as far as water is concerned. They have had the opportunity to sink their roots deep into the soil without disturbance or damage and they are out in the garden getting as much rain as comes their way. The earlier they are sown, the better, as there is likely to be more rain in spring and early summer to get them going, than later on. Unless the soil is already very wet or heavy rain is forecast, water seeds in well after planting them. Use a hose or watering can with a reasonably fine spray attachment so you don't water them out of the ground again.

From late spring onwards, if the weather is dry for more than about a week, you will need to water outdoor plants every couple of days. This depends on your soil type: clay soil can be left slightly longer than sandy soil. Sometimes a dry-looking crust forms on the surface but the ground underneath is still quite damp. If in doubt, dig down with a trowel to have a look.

Plants under cover

Plants grown in pots for planting out, or those in the greenhouse or cold frame, rely entirely on you for their water, so you must be assiduous in your care. Check them daily and water with a hose or watering can; have the water running gently and wet the compost not the foliage. It is almost inevitable that from time to time you will fall short of expectations and come home to trays of wilted seedlings. But don't despair – most will rally, as long as it doesn't happen on a regular basis. Be careful not to overwater as this is as harmful as underwatering: if you're not sure, lift the pot to feel how heavy it is and push your finger an inch or two down into the compost. You'll soon get to know if it needs water or not.

Planting out pot-grown seedlings

When you plant them into the vegetable garden, pot-grown seedlings will need a good watering to soak them and the surrounding soil. This beds them in well and encourages their roots to leave the potting compost. Check and water them regularly until you can see they are growing away.

Seedbed plants

Vegetables raised in seedbeds have a bit of a hard time of it at transplanting time. There they are happily established with a nice set of roots, and then someone comes along and hoicks them out. No matter how careful you are, you will damage some roots. So such transplants need as much, if not more, care in their watering than those raised in pots.

Chilli plants like plenty of water, but don't want to stand in it. Terracotta pots ensure drainage and airflow, but they do need regular attention.

Going on holiday?

It's one of life's ironies that the holiday season coincides with the time when there is prolific growth in the garden and (in most years, at least) not much rain. Ensuring your plants will get enough water while you are away on holiday can be a bit of a headache.

■ If you are going for a week, water the vegetable garden well beforehand and ask a friend or neighbour just to water your pots and plants undercover. No two people water in the same way, so don't blame them if they don't get it exactly 'right'. Be glad they did it anyway – they won't do too much damage in a week.

■ For longer periods, use a seeper hose system with a timer to water the veg beds regularly. The disadvantage of this is that it will come on even if it's pouring with rain. However, unless you have very heavy soil, this won't hurt anything but your water bill. For plants in pots and undercover, a trickle system of watering is ideal, if fiddly to install, and you can make use of it even when you are at home. Alternatively, use capillary matting.

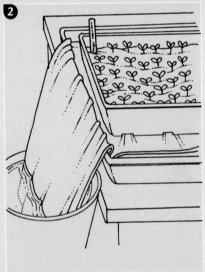

For plants that are growing under cover, you can rig up one of the following automatic watering systems for hot days and holidays:

① Trickle system. With this, a timer is fixed to a tap. The timer is set to allow water to drip through narrow tubes into each plant pot for a few hours every day.

② Capillary matting. This is placed in a tray under plant pots or trays of seedlings, with the end dangling in a bucket of water. The matting soaks up the water, drawing it continuously into the tray. It is an efficient system, but you do have to replenish the bucket every now and then to ensure that the matting never dries out.

Feeding

Even when you have lovingly prepared their living quarters with compost, well-rotted muck and chicken manure pellets (or whatever else you favour), some of your vegetable plants will get hungry. Remember that veg grow very fast once they get going, so this isn't really the time to be using slow-release fertilizers (*see* page 29, although they will serve to keep up the overall fertility of the soil). The most common way to boost plants in full growth is with liquid or soluble feeds. These are absorbed instantly with water and are ideal for feeding vegetable plants in containers, too.

How much and how often?

It doesn't take much imagination to realize that what can be watered in can also be watered out: liquid feeds don't hang around in the soil for long. If the plant doesn't make immediate use of them, the rain or your watering will wash them away. This is why the slow-release merchants are better in the long term. Some particularly hungry vegetables, and those grown in containers, need to have a regular schedule of feeding that is weekly or, in some cases, more frequently; others are content with a couple of good meals in the growing season. The A–Z will inform you of the specific requirements of the vegetables you are growing.

Making a choice

There is a huge variety of fertilizers, and, again, making a decision about which one to use comes down to whether or not you want to be organic. If you need some help to make up your mind, go along to your garden centre and have a read of some of the boxes and bottles; there are also many websites that include information on the subject.

The following are available in liquid and/or soluble form:

Tomatoes are demanding and greedy and you can easily tell a well-fed plant – large, rich-green leaves and fat, shiny, juicy tomatoes – from one that is going hungry – small, yellowing and sometimes curling leaves and small, hard tomatoes.

Seaweed extract This organic and sustainable liquid feed is high in nitrogen (N) and trace elements (*see* box, page 29). It is used in a very diluted form and is a great tonic when sprayed on as a foliar feed.

Tomato feed This is specifically formulated for tomatoes, but can be used on any fruiting plants. It is a good source of potash (K) and magnesium. The most widely available brands are not organic, but organic versions are available.

General-purpose feed Higher in nitrogen (N) than potash (K), this is intended for use on fast-growing leafy crops, like salads. Organic suppliers stock organic alternatives.

Epsom salts These are a source of magnesium and can be used for treating obvious deficiencies, particularly in tomatoes.

Fish emulsion An underused organic product, this has an NPK of 5-2-2, plus trace elements. Like seaweed extract, it is used very diluted and releases its nutrients quickly to benefit a wide range of vegetables. It is a great tonic early in the growing season when slow-release fertilizers are only just getting going.

Home-made liquid feeds

If you are keen to be as organic as possible, it is relatively simple and inexpensive to produce liquid feeds from the leaves of comfrey, stinging nettles, or borage. Such feeds are rich in potassium (K) and nitrogen (N) and are excellent for tomatoes

and for helping plants to resist disease.

Collect the leaves (all of one type, or mixed), pack them into a fine-mesh sack and put them in a watertight container, preferably something like a small barrel or waterbutt which has a tap near the bottom. Cover with water (some people advocate adding some human urine, too). After a few weeks the whole lot will have rotted to produce a (really) stinky liquid that you dilute to the colour of weak tea before using on your vegetable patch (use as often as you would use other liquid feeds, depending on the vegetable involved). As these feeds have not been concocted under a microscope, the nutrient levels will vary, so keep an eye on the health of your plants to ensure they really are getting all they need.

A waterbutt is ideal for comfrey feed. Put the leaves in a fine mesh sack so their rotted remains won't block the tap and are easier to remove.

Nettle feed can be made in an open tub, as long as you don't mind the smell. The resulting liquid is high in nitrogen.

It's not by chance that the most widely available liquid plant foods are those called 'tomato feed', as tomatoes do need plenty of food. However, lots of other vegetables benefit from a liquid tomato feed. Never add 'one for the pot'.

Weeding

No sooner have you got your vegetable patch neatly dug and raked over than the weeds move in. Countless generations of them have lived and seeded in this soil; they have long-since adapted to thriving in local conditions; and they are tough and resourceful – you might admire their detemination, but they are the enemy.

Why weed?

If you are tempted to say, 'Well, there's plenty of space, why not let them grow?', think again. Weeds don't just look bad: they need to be kept under control for various reasons:

■ They grow fast, smothering small seedlings, which then die from lack of light and space.
■ They help to harbour pests, such as slugs and snails, which will then feed on your crops.
■ Some suffer from the same diseases as vegetables, such as clubroot and rusts, so can be a source of problems.
■ They compete with crops for water and feed, which can mean the difference between good crops and poor crops – or no crops at all.

Annual weeds:
① Chickweed.
② Annual meadow grass.
③ Goosegrass or cleavers.
④ Speedwell.

Perennial weeds:
⑤ Hogweed.
⑥ Japanese knotweed.

Beating weeds

If you have done your soil preparation work well (*see* page 32), you will be in a position to get the better of most of these interlopers. Do it sooner rather than later, and the job will take no time at all. Annual weeds and small perennial weeds can be dealt with by hoeing; larger, deep-rooted perennial weeds may require more effort.

While the weed seedlings are still tiny and your crops are still small, hoe every week or two. For best results, hoe on a dry, sunny day and leave the weed seedlings to shrivel up in the sun.

When the weeds are a bit bigger you can still hoe them out, but it takes longer and you need to clear them away afterwards, otherwise they can root back into the soil, especially in showery weather.

If the weeds are well on their way to adulthood, you will have to dig them out individually. Don't leave it a second longer; if they are allowed to seed, you are looking at next year's problem. Digging out takes a lot longer than hoeing and there's always the risk of prompting the weeds to seed as you disturb them – hairy bittercress is particularly prone to springing its seeds when touched. When digging out, you may also disturb veg roots near the surface or accidentally pull out the odd veg plant as well.

The good news is that most veg crops only need hoeing at the start of their life. Once they grow big enough to shade the soil between rows, they will largely smother annual weeds, so you only need to whip out the odd one that struggles through. But slender plants, such as onions and leeks, never create enough shade to do the job, so you will need to set aside time to hoe them regularly from sowing or planting right through until you harvest them. Space them a hoe's width apart when you plant them!

Perennial weeds

In some ways, perennial weeds are less of a problem in a vegetable patch than they are in an ornamental garden. Because of the constant soil disturbance they don't have a chance to really take hold. On the other hand, this very soil disturbance can break up their roots, which effectively propagates many of them (*see* Rotavators, page 26).

The best way to remove perennial weeds, which include bindweed, ground elder, dandelions, docks and stinging nettles, is to dig them up,

① Ground elder (perennial).   ② Dandelion (perennial).   ③ Dock (perennial).

roots and all. Easy to say: almost impossible to do. Most root very deeply and have brittle roots that annoyingly snap just below your trowel. Leaving just the bare minimum behind will enable them to re-grow. You have three choices:

■ Revisit each weed on a regular basis (weekly), removing all top growth. This will weaken and eventually kill it.

■ Use a spot weedkiller. Based on glyphosate, these are painted or sprayed on the offending plant and nothing else. They are not for committed organic gardeners and may need several applications (*see also* page 33), but they do work.

■ Use a flame-gun. Again, this needs to be done regularly to ensure the root is killed off. For obvious reasons the flame gun has to be used before your vegetable seedlings emerge.

Small patches of weeds can be removed with a trowel, especially where they have got rather too large to hoe off.

④ Stinging nettle (perennial).

⑤ Thistle (usually perennial; some species are annual or biennial).

⑥ Bramble (perennial).

Pests and diseases

One day you are pottering among your vegetables full of pride at how well they are all doing, and the next day something or someone has had a go at them. The trouble with pests and diseases is that they are quite discreet about their presence until they really get a hold, and they can go through a crop like a cold through a primary school. Years ago, gardeners would have reached for a spray gun, but we now realize that most of the chemical weapons we have to kill pests and diseases kill indiscriminately. As well as dispatching pests and diseases, they are potentially harmful to all the useful wildlife and other organisms in the garden, as well as to humans, too. For these reasons, many modern gardeners prefer to avoid using them.

Netting cabbages is an environmentally friendly way to protect your crop from pigeons and cabbage white butterflies.

So what's the solution?
Fortunately, there are effective ways to reduce the impact of plant problems; from simply ensuring your crops are in the peak of health to be able to resist disease, to using barriers and eco-friendly controls to ward off unwanted bugs.

Keep your plants healthy
Hearty, vigorous, unstressed plants can shrug off the loss of a couple of leaves, and cope with one or two greenfly settling on them. Boost their immune systems by practising crop rotation (see page 23) and good growing techniques and feeding regularly, particularly with seaweed extract (see page 48).

Remove pests by hand The larger, visible pests, such as snails, slugs, caterpillars and various aphids, are easy to remove by hand. Dispatch them by squashing, cutting in half, or feeding them to your hens or ducks.

Use physical barriers Fine-mesh netting can be used to protect almost any vegetable plants in their early days. It is particularly useful for carrots, which can be martyrs to carrot fly. Lay it over the seed drills as soon as you have sown the seeds, burying its edges under the soil. You will need to remove it for weeding, but water will go right through it. The mesh can be left over smaller plants for their whole lives – it is light

The robin is a great pest-eating ally in the vegetable garden.

enough to be lifted by them as they grow – but larger ones will outgrow it, by which time they should be safer from pests anyway.

Birds are fond of various crops in the garden, such as peas and brassicas. To discourage them you may need to build low-level protective cages over the objects of their desire, using metal hoops and bird netting, but do make sure they are impenetrable or birds may become trapped and injure themselves.

Use companion plants
Companion plants are the fall guys of the vegetable garden. They are there to distract all the unpleasant characters from your veg. There are various theories about how they work, the two main ones being that the pests find them more attractive than the veg, or that they disguise the smell of some vegetables, effectively throwing the pests off-course.

Good companions

① French marigolds are attractive to a wide variety of beneficial insects, while their strong smell may distract pests from your main crops.

② Nasturtiums are popular with vegetable gardeners and pests alike – particularly black fly (aphids) and cabbage white butterflies.

DISTRACTION TACTICS

The following are often planted for their reputed ability to mask the scent of your crops (thereby preventing pests from locating them) or for attractiveness to pests (thereby distracting them from your crops).

Herbs (such as chervil, chives, dill, hyssop, lavender, thyme) produce distracting scent. They offer another benefit in that they attract pollinators to the vegetable garden, which increases yields.

Basil deters whitefly from tomatoes.

French marigold roots exude chemicals that reduce the numbers of pest nematodes, slugs and wireworms.

Nasturtiums attract aphids away from broad beans, and cabbage white butterflies away from brassica crops.

GOOD MATES

Some plants seem to do better grown together than separately, but companion planting doesn't seem to work for all gardeners. This inconsistency may be to do with variability in the density of planting and the fact that people experience different growing conditions. If you are interested in companion planting it is worth experimenting with the following combinations to see what works for you:

- Beetroot, chard, beans, brassicas, onion family (alliums), parsnips.
- Brassicas, French beans, onion family, potatoes, tomatoes.
- Carrots, runner beans, onion family, peas, tomatoes.
- Onion family, beetroot, brassicas, carrots, lettuce, tomatoes.
- Runner beans, carrots, sweetcorn, peas.
- Spinach, lettuce, peas, radish.

Use biological controls Almost every insect is on the hitlist of another insect, the main reasons being it provides an excellent meal, or it makes the perfect nursery for incubating young. Scientists have made of study of pests and their nemeses, and have developed ways of bringing the two together for the benefit of the vegetable gardener. If you have a persistent problem with a pest in the list (*see* box), you can purchase its biological control from a specialist supplier.

Live with some things Pests and diseases are a fact of life and do not always have to spell complete disaster for your crops. Some problems are more prevalent in particular areas or soils, or during some types of weather conditions, often when it is damp or very wet in summer. Most often the damage they do is limited and you could simply resign yourself to sharing a proportion of your crops with them. If you suffer repeated crop failures, then consider carefully whether it is worth growing that particular vegetable, or try a different approach. For example, potatoes can get blight in late summer if the weather is persistently wet. Grow the early-maturing varieties of potato (*see* page 102) instead, which you harvest before blight is around, thus avoiding the problem.

Pest/Biological control

All biological controls must be used according to the manufacturer's instructions and will only work for a limited amount of time. Of those listed, only the slug and wireworm nematodes (microscopic eelworms) are suitable for outdoor use in the veg garden.

PEST	BIOLOGICAL CONTROL
Whitefly	wasp larva *Encarsia formosa*
Red spider mite	*Phytosieulus persimilis*
Vine weevil	nematode *Steinernema kraussei*
Slugs	nematode *Phasmarhabditis hermaphrodita*
Wireworms	nematode *Heterorhabditis megadis*

Know the enemy

In combating pests and diseases it pays to be prepared with a plan of attack even before they appear.

Slugs and snails

These are a continuous problem, particularly serious on young vegetable plants, which can disappear overnight. Use a selection of the various remedies below in and around the veg garden, beginning a few weeks before sowing or planting, to reduce numbers overall.

Keep them at bay

■ Natural predators include thrushes, hedgehogs (don't we all wish we had one resident), newts, frogs and toads, and ground beetles.
■ Copper tape is best fixed round the outside of raised veg beds and pots; it delivers a slight electric shock.
■ Absorbent granules dehydrate slugs and snails so they can't glide along.
■ Yucca extract or garlic-based deterrents taste bitter.
■ Sharp grit and prickly leaves, such as holly, have a limited effect.
■ Beer traps made from yoghurt pots or jam jars sunk into the ground are quite effective – lager is a favourite.
■ Biological controls (*see* box, page 53).
■ Hand picking is particularly effective with snails, but they must be destroyed; they will return if you simply throw them next door.

Aphids

Greenfly and blackfly are mainly a problem in spring. They are mostly found near the tips of soft young shoots and on the undersides of young leaves. A small infestation won't do much harm, though a larger one can weaken plants; they may spread virus diseases.

Keep them at bay

■ Natural predators include blue tits and other birds, hoverflies, ladybirds, lacewings, spiders and several species of parasitic wasp, so encourage these into your garden.
■ Squash them between your fingertips or use a damp tissue or cotton wool.
■ Fine-mesh covers will discourage them if used early enough.
■ Spray with an organic remedy. Check to make sure it's suitable for edible plants.

Soil pests

Soil pests strike underground or just below the soil surface. Wireworms are shiny, yellow-orange maggots. They bore into roots, such as potatoes, causing early rotting. Cutworms shear the roots from the plants – your first clue will be wilting in the crop. They are fat, greyish caterpillars curled into a C shape.

Keep them at bay

Soil pests are mostly a problem in veg beds cultivated on sites that were once grassland. This means that good soil preparation and allowing time for birds and wildlife to pick off the worst of the soil pests over winter is all the more important. Hens and ducks will be glad to oblige, too. Black beetles feed on cabbage root fly larvae and other pests, as do centipedes. You could collect them up and let them loose around the brassicas.

Caterpillars

Caterpillars are voracious feeders, and cabbage white caterpillars (offspring of both large and small white butterflies) are notorious for stripping the leaves of brassicas.

Keep them at bay

■ Natural predators such as blackbirds and robins will take small caterpillars, and even wasps will do so early in the season.
■ Check susceptible plants regularly and remove caterpillars or suspect clusters of eggs on the undersides of leaves by hand.
■ Fine-mesh covers will prevent butterflies laying eggs on brassica leaves if used early enough.

Blight – potato and tomato

Affected plants develop brown spots, especially round the edges of the leaves, and these quickly spread throughout the entire crop. If not  treated swiftly, the stems turn brown, dry out and shrivel up. Similarly, tomato plants turn brown and dry out and the tomatoes develop brown rotting patches on the fruit. Potatoes develop scabby cankers with brown patches inside the tubers, which soon rot.

Keep it at bay

■ Blight is common particularly in damp summers, and once it arrives on your potatoes or tomatoes it is too late to do anything, so if there is rain in mid- to late summer, spray fortnightly with Bordeaux mixture before the problem arises.

■ If you experience an outbreak of blight, don't put foliage, fruit, tubers or peelings from affected plants onto the compost heap. Burn them or remove them from your site. Next year, plant early-maturing potato plants (blight is more likely to

develop later in the growing season) and select blight-resistant tomato and potato varieties.

Fungal infections

Grey mould or botrytis is a common problem in greenhouses and polytunnels, especially early in the year when conditions are cold, dull and damp, and where ventilation is poor. It can affect leaves,  flowers and fruit: it is responsible for the translucent 'ghost spots' that can appear on green or red tomatoes.

'Damping off' is a distressing fungal infection of young seedlings, as they suddenly collapse and die without warning. Outdoors, fungal infections may also cause problems. Members of the onion family – garlic and leeks – can suffer from rust; the leaves develop red-brown spots. Although annoying, rust is not as bad as the dreaded white rot, which also affects the onion family. The leaves turn yellow, and then fluffy, white moulds develop at the bases of the plants. This fungus kills your crop and is very persistent in the soil.

Keep them at bay

■ Improve ventilation in greenhouses and polytunnels as a preventive measure.

■ Use very clean pots and trays for planting seeds.

■ Water seedlings regularly with Cheshunt compound (copper-based fungicide) to prevent damping off.

■ General-purpose fungicides are available that fight against botrytis. If you do resort to chemicals, check that the product is suitable for edible crops of the type you are going to treat.

■ Rust and white rot are not treatable and are best avoided by practising good crop rotation.

Viruses

There are many virus diseases, most of which reveal themselves in blotching, marbling or yellowing of the plant foliage. Viruses will affect the vigour of the plant and so its ability to crop well and produce good yields.

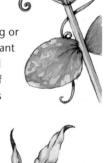

Keep them at bay

■ There are no cures to virus diseases. Destroy affected plants by burning them or by removing infected crops from the site, and keep greenfly under control to prevent any viruses from spreading amongst veg crops.

Most vegetables grow happily in well-prepared garden soil, needing only regular water supplies and the odd boost of something nutritious from the gardener. However, there is a significant minority of tall veg plants that require support.

Every vegetable gardener will amass a good collection of bamboo canes and other sticks and stakes on which to cosset and train the lax, loose-limbed plants in his or her care. There are numerous individual methods of constructing supports and tying in plants, but here are a few standard rules:

Canes

These are needed for climbing French and runner beans. Each plant needs a tall cane or length of twine to twist around. Canes are either set in a long row or in a wigwam (*see* illustration). The beans may need help and a bit of guidance at first,

but they will soon put out tendrils that will seek out and start to wind around the poles. Bear in mind that native hazel bean poles are more environmentally friendly than bamboo canes, which will have been shipped halfway across the world.

Stakes

Use stakes to support cordon tomatoes, cucumbers and aubergines. Push the stake into the ground beside the plant when it is still quite small, and tie the stem to it as it grows. Don't tie the knots too tight, and check them all regularly to ensure they aren't strangling the plant and damaging new growth.

Peasticks can be made from the prunings of any woody plant that has plenty of side branches and twiggy growth.

Three or four canes tied together at the top to form a wigwam make the perfect climbing frame for runner beans.

Use soft gardener's twine to tie tomatoes to supports. Ensure the tie is stable by crossing the twine between plant and stake, to make a figure of eight.

Peasticks

Peas are wonderful for sprawling, straggly plants. Hazel and birch twigs are favourites. The taller varieties of broad bean also need help. You can't tie them up neatly, just give them something to lean on and coil around. Sticks with plenty of thin twiggy branches offer good support for pea plants. Alternatively, push in bamboo canes or finger-thick hazel stems on either side of the row and link them with soft twine to corral the crop.

Protection falls into three categories: to provide extra warmth, to protect from cold, and to protect from pests. In practice, the first two come down to the same thing – sheltering the plants from extremes of weather using a greenhouse, cold frame, cloche or gardener's fleece, at various stages of their lives or throughout their lives, or to extend the growing season, so making either earlier sowing or later harvesting possible. For protection from pests, *see* pages 52–5. The A–Z of Vegetables, which begins on page 60, has more information on all plants in the lists below.

① Planting tomatoes and cucumbers in a greenhouse border.

② Sturdy plastic cloches are easy to move around to where needed.

③ A fine-mesh cloche acts as a temporary barrier against a wide variety of pests.

④ By protecting mizuna salad leaves with fleece, you can extend its season.

Protection chart

NAME	PROTECT FROM COLD AND LATE FROST	PROVIDE CONTINUOUS PROTECTION	GROW UNDER COVER FOR AN EARLY CROP	START UNDER COVER FOR PLANTING OUT LATER	GROW UNDER COVER FOR A LONGER SEASON
Aubergines [1]	■	■		■	
Beetroot			■		■
Beans, broad				■	■
Beans, French	■			■	
Beans, runner	■			■	
Brussels sprouts		■		■	
Cabbages – summer and autumn varieties				■	
Calabrese				■	
Cauliflower – summer and autumn varieties				■	
Celeriac				■	
Celery				■	
Chillies [2]	■	■		■	
Courgettes	■			■	
Cucumbers [2]	■	■		■	
Florence fennel			■	■	
Lettuces	■		■	■	■
Peas					■
Peppers [1,2]	■	■		■	
Pumpkins and squashes	■			■	
Radishes			■		■
Salad leaves (some)			■	■	■
Sweetcorn	■			■	
Tomatoes [2]	■	■		■	
Turnips			■		■

[1] Can be grown outside in a sheltered spot, but success is more likely with continuous protection.
[2] There are indoor and outdoor varieties, all need initial protection from cold.

Storage

When you grow vegetables there are times when you have far more produce to harvest than you are able to eat. Runner beans and courgettes, lettuce and other salad leaves all go through a phase in mid- to late summer when it takes a very determined vegetable-eater to keep on top of their proliferation. So, although the best time to eat vegetables is within minutes of picking them – which is why we grow them, of course – you might need to find ways of putting them aside for enjoyment later. The A–Z of Vegetables (*see* pages 60–117) also provides some useful information on ways to store each individual type of vegetable.

Onions don't need to be plaited together in order to store well, but it is a good way to ensure they are well ventilated and out of the damp. They look attractive, too, but avoid too much warmth or they may dehydrate.

In the shed

Most root vegetables (Jerusalem artichokes, beetroots, carrots, celeriac, parsnips) can be left in the ground until they are needed or the weather turns very wet. If the weather does turn wet, these roots will keep (cleaned and dried) in a cool shed for a while, but don't leave them in there and forget about them. Check them regularly for signs of mould or rodent damage and use them as quickly as possible.

If you want to store them for a long time, put unblemished, unwashed root vegetables in a box of slightly damp sand – make sure they are not touching – and cover them over. This keeps the flesh firm.

Maincrop potatoes and onions tend to be harvested all at once in fairly large numbers. They keep perfectly well in a cool shed or garage. Garlic needs to be stored in slightly warmer conditions, though still cool, in the house. With all these, it is vital to make sure they are completely dry on the outside, with most of the soil brushed off, before storage. Potatoes are fine in paper or hessian sacks, while onions and garlic can be plaited to hang up, or stored on trays. Don't store any produce that is bruised or damaged: it will quickly rot and could spoil the rest of your harvest.

If you don't have a cool shed, use the coolest room in the house. Potatoes need to be kept in the dark to prevent them from sprouting; onions and garlic in the light.

In the kitchen

It is always better by far to pick vegetables and salads as required so that you always eat them fresh. But if you do need to store them, the best storage place is the salad drawer of the fridge. Most will keep there for a few days, and they will still be fresher than their supermarket counterparts.

Freezing

Most vegetables can be frozen. Many lose their texture and some of their flavour in the process, but this might be better than throwing them away.

Freezing is fine for broad beans and peas, as long as you do it as soon as you have picked them. Blanch them first: immerse them in boiling water for a minute or two and then plunge them into cold water and dry well before freezing.

If you have huge numbers of courgettes and tomatoes, they can be frozen, but the former are better frozen within a cooked dish, such as ratatouille, and the latter as a purée to be added to sauces, stews or pasta dishes, when defrosted.

With any veg, don't freeze any specimens that are less than perfect – they won't improve with time – and use all frozen vegetables within a few months as they still go on deteriorating in the freezer.

Juicing fresh vegetables

One of the healthiest ways of using surplus fresh produce is to invest in a juicer and convert tomatoes, carrots, beetroot and cucumbers into drinks, which can be as delicious as they are colourful. Drink these straight away, though:

vitamins are soon lost as the juice oxidizes, and it quickly changes colour or goes cloudy and then looks much less appetizing.

Green tomato chutney

This mild, sweetish chutney is lovely with mature cheddar and cold meat, and it's the perfect way to use up tomatoes that you know have no hope of turning red.

1.4kg (3lb) green tomatoes
14g (½oz) salt
113g (4oz) sultanas
170g (6oz) chopped onion
170g (6oz) chopped apple
170g (6oz) sugar
14g (½oz) mustard seed
½ teaspoon pepper
½ teaspoon pickling spice
425ml (¾ pint) white vinegar

Chop or mince the green tomatoes and put them into a basin in layers, sprinkling each with salt. Cover and leave to stand overnight. Drain and discard the liquid from the tomatoes, then put all the ingredients into a pan and cook slowly until you obtain a soft pulp. This takes about two hours. Pot the chutney into sterilized jam jars.

Storing tomatoes

If you have plenty of tomatoes at the end of the summer you could also try drying them in the oven (have it on the very lowest setting for a couple of hours with the door just ajar). However, it might be more satisfying and energy-saving to create your own tomato ketchup, chutneys and pickles, to which you could even add other surplus veg. These are easy to make and keep for a long time, although the original flavour of the vegetable will be masked to a greater or lesser extent.

Vegetables can be made into chutneys, jellies and a wide variety of preserves. This pumpkin preserve was made using lemons, sugar, salt and mixed spices.

A–Z of Vegetables

In this A–Z, each description provides the key cultivation needs of the vegetable and any special requirements it may have. For example, many plants can be started off in pots indoors, but some are better planted where they are to grow (in situ) because they dislike having their roots disturbed. Watering and weeding are mentioned many times. They are the two most important aspects of vegetable gardening and shouldn't be neglected: weed when you're feeling energetic, water when you simply want some peaceful time out in the garden. And don't forget to water every pot-raised plant before and after you plant it out into the garden, even if the soil is already damp – this is vital.

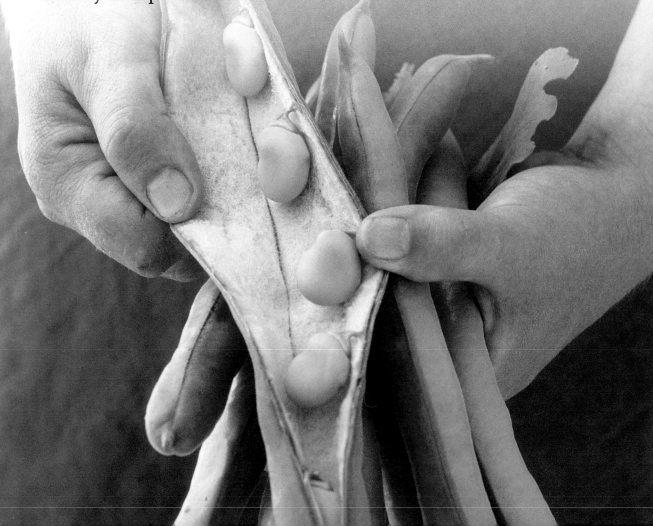

Making choices

There are some vegetables – potatoes, beans, tomatoes, lettuce – that you can be sure of finding in almost every vegetable garden up and down the country. These plants are the backbone of the veg garden: they usually grow well, they always taste good, and with a bit of effort they will produce a worthwhile crop. The A–Z describes them and how best to grow them. However, it also includes some of the more borderline creatures, such as aubergine, celery and Florence fennel, which can be a challenge and require additional cossetting and nurturing, but are worth trying if you like to eat them, as home-grown ones will always taste better than the shop-bought variety – even if they're only half the size. Some of the veg featured will do better with a little protection, and with others it is undeniable that a greenhouse or polytunnel will achieve larger yields, but on the whole you should be able to grow those featured in normal or sheltered garden conditions.

What's in a name?

Nowadays there is a huge and wonderful selection of vegetable seeds available from many different suppliers, so it can be difficult to make a choice. Within each vegetable description in the A–Z there are suggestions of particular varieties of vegetables you might like to try and grow, but if you can't find those mentioned when you are buying seed, rest assured that the majority of seeds on the market have been carefully bred to be reliable and tasty, or they have proved their worth over many years. As long as you read the catalogue or seed packet description carefully, like what you read, and it suits your growing conditions, you can't go far wrong.

Which ones to grow in pots?

Of the vegetables featured in the A–Z, only asparagus and globe artichokes are totally unsuitable for growing in containers, although no doubt somebody somewhere will be doing it successfully. This is because they are perennial plants, which means that they need lots of space to grow and time to establish before they crop well, by which time they'll have outgrown their pot. Of the rest, some are better than others for growing in containers, simply because of their particular cropping habits.

From a 'time and motion' point of view, the best plants to choose for containers are those that crop over a longish period, such as tomatoes, peppers and runner beans, or that are quick to mature, such as radishes, lettuce and other salad leaves. There are also the squash and marrow family, which do quite well in growbags, as long as there is space in the surrounding area for them to stretch out. Alternatively, you could train squashes and marrows up strong supports; there are varieties bred for just such a purpose. Potatoes are famous for their adaptability. Two or three seed potatoes (*see* pages 102–4) can be planted in a compost bag to produce a good crop with little work.

HOW IS IT DONE?
Fill the containers with a mixture of good, soilless, multipurpose compost and soil-based potting compost – half and half is a good start.

Plant larger vegetables, such as tomatoes, peppers and aubergines, individually in containers, and smaller ones, such as some chillies, two or three to a pot. Salad vegetables are best in wide shallow(ish) pots or boxes, as these will provide more leaf-growing space without taking up too much potting compost. Long root vegetables need deeper pots but can be planted quite densely. Beans, both French and runner, can be planted in groups 10cm (4in) apart in tubs or growbags. Provide them with an obelisk or wigwam of canes for support, or position them to grow up a trellis or netting against a fence or wall. Given shelter, they will do very well. Alternatively, you could choose dwarf varieties of beans, which won't need as much support, but will produce a smaller crop.

Aubergines do well planted in generous-sized pots. The plant has hairy leaves and spiky fruit stems. It is a member of the potato family with very similar-looking flowers.

Artichokes, Globe

SOW MAR, APR **plant** APR
harvest JUL, AUG, SEP

Globe artichokes are grown for their tasty flowerbuds, and make excellent ornamental plants, too. They have silvery leaves that are cut like a thistle's and they reach up to 1.5m (5ft) tall. One or two plants are enough for the average family. If you don't get around to eating all the buds before the flowers open, the bees will thank you.

Though not the best for flavour, 'Green Globe' is a reliable cropper producing big flower buds. It is common and widely available as seed and plants.

Cultivation

DIFFICULTY Easy; low input.
SOW under cover in late winter or in an outdoor seedbed in early spring.
PLANT out in mid-spring. Also sold as young plants.
SPACE 90cm (3ft) apart with 90cm–1.2m (3–4ft) between rows.
CARE Summer – water during dry spells when plants are carrying a crop. Mid-spring – feed each plant with slow-release fertilizer and mulch generously. Autumn – cut down old stems as plants die down. No supports needed.
YIELD Six to ten buds per plant each season.
STORAGE Artichokes will keep for a week in the salad drawer of the fridge.

Keep them happy by...

Providing a warm, sunny, sheltered spot in well-drained soil. Allow them a year to establish before you start harvesting, but don't allow flowers to develop during the first summer – snip off buds as soon as you see them. Replace plants every four to five years; in year three, pot up some of the small offsets that form round their base to start a new establishing row the following year.

Worth trying...

'Gros Camus de Bretagne' – French variety, hard to find as plants. Flavour is superb from very large heads.
'Gros Vert de Lâon' – French variety, widely available as plants. Good flavour.
'Violetto di Chioggia' – Available as seed or plants with pretty mauve buds. Fair flavour but lightish crops.

Enjoy them...

From midsummer to early autumn. Harvest half-grown (fist-sized) flower buds, using secateurs to snip through the stem about 2.5cm (1in) below the base of the bud.

Look out for...

Blackfly often attack artichoke flower buds; a light attack is no problem as the outer scales are removed before cooking, but a bad infestation is very off-putting on the plate. If you see blackfly while crops are growing, wipe them off developing buds with a damp cloth or a soft brush dipped in water. Earwigs can also be a problem. Soak the flower buds upside-down in salted water before cooking to remove them.

Artichokes, Jerusalem

plant FEB, MAR
harvest JAN, FEB, MAR AND OCT, NOV, DEC

Jerusalem artichokes are grown for their plump knobbly tubers, which are baked, fried, roasted or stewed, just like potatoes. The plants are weatherproof, even though the stems reach 3m (10ft) high, and low-maintenance, so they make a good allotment crop.

Cultivation

DIFFICULTY Very easy; low input.

PLANT egg-sized tubers 15cm (6in) deep in late winter or early spring. Save some of the best tubers from each crop to plant next year.

SPACE 40cm (15in) apart, with 90cm (3ft) between rows. Plant a double or triple row so these tall plants can support each other. This also makes a good windbreak.

CARE Use a general fertilizer when preparing the soil; no extra watering or feeding is needed. Flower buds can be removed to increase tuber yield, but in practise this is unnecessary as the yields are high, and the sunflower-like flowers are a bonus.

YIELD 2kg (4lb) per tuber planted.

STORAGE Leave them in the ground until they're wanted, as they store better there than anywhere else.

Keep them happy by...

Staking in a windy site or, if you must be neat, bang in a stake each end of a row and run long strings or plastic-coated wire either side of the plants. You'll have a bigger crop if you earth up the plants when they've reached about 45cm (18in) high.

Worth trying...

'Fuseau' – Less knobbly tubers than normal, which are easier to clean and peel for cooking.

Enjoy them...

From mid-autumn right through winter. When the plants start dying off in autumn, cut them back to 30cm (12in) high, after which you can simply dig up individual plants any time you want some tubers. Tubers still in the ground the following mid-spring will start growing again, so use them before then.

Look out for...

Save some of the best tubers to re-plant next year.

The distinctive knobbly tubers of Jerusalem artichokes. They make nourishing and flavoursome winter soups.

HOW TO earth up

Earthing up Jerusalem artichokes and potatoes encourages the shoots to root and boosts tuber production. With asparagus and celery it keeps the stems pale and tender.

1 Plant the vegetable as normal and wait until shoots start to appear, then use a draw hoe to pull the soil up and over them and block out the light.

2 The shoots will reappear and when they are about 15cm (6in) high, cover their lower half again, then leave the plants to develop normally.

Asparagus

plant APR
harvest APR, MAY, JUN

Asparagus is pricey in the shops, to say nothing of being well travelled, so it is worth growing it yourself to enjoy it when it is really fresh. On the downside, it is a perennial and needs plenty of space. You buy it as 'crowns' from specialist growers who have raised these for several years already. It still needs a further three years to settle in to your veg bed before you get much of a harvest, but the plants may then continue cropping for 8–20 years.

Cultivation

DIFFICULTY Easy; medium input.
PLANT each crown in a generous hole, spread the roots out well then cover with 5cm (2in) of soil. Water well. As shoots start to appear above the ground, gradually earth up the plants until they are growing along ridges up to 15cm (6in) high.
SPACE 30–45cm (12–18in) apart, with 90cm (3ft) between each row.
CARE In early to mid-spring, sprinkle general fertilizer over the asparagus beds; water if the weather is very dry during the cropping season. Hand-weed beds regularly; don't use a fork for removing weeds – asparagus plants are shallow rooted and dislike disturbance.
YIELD About 20–25 spears per mature plant.
STORAGE Don't store – eat fresh!

Keep them happy by...

Planting crowns in well-drained ground or in slightly raised beds on their own, adding plenty of organic matter during the previous winter.

Do not cut any emerging spears for the first two summers after planting, and then only take a light crop in the first few weeks of the cutting season in year three. From then on you can harvest as much as you like until early summer. In autumn, cut the yellowed or browning fern to 5cm (2in) above ground, then weed and mulch the soil generously with well-rotted organic matter.

Worth trying...

'Connover's Colossal' – An old favourite, readily available as both male and female plants – females are less prolific and shed

Thick, sturdy asparagus spears emerging from a gravel mulch, which will discourage slugs snacking on them. They are regarded as the elite among vegetables, and though it takes three years for a bed to come into regular cropping, the results will amply repay your patience.

seed via berries that ripen towards autumn; self-sown seedlings are a nuisance.

'Jersey Giant' – Long-season variety, cropping two weeks earlier than most and continuing to early summer.

'Jersey Knight' – Vigorous, heavy-cropping, all-male F1 hybrid, readily available from the mail-order firms. Thick spears and superb flavour.

'Stewart's Purple' – For those who like colour; sweet-tasting, purple spears from mid-spring.

Enjoy them...

From mid-spring to early summer. Cut spears as soon as they reach about 15cm (6in) tall. Use a strong knife to cut them off 5cm (2in) below the soil surface and then refill the hole with soil to prevent pests from getting in. After early summer, let the plants grow and complete their life cycle.

Look out for...

Self-sown asparagus seedlings grow quickly and are soon indistinguishable from those with pedigrees, except in their output, which is generally much poorer. These interlopers then overcrowd beds, reducing the yield from your chosen variety.

Thin asparagus spears usually come from weak plants that have been cropped too early, cut too heavily in previous years, or not fed sufficiently – or all three.

Slugs also like emerging spears (*see* pages 52–5 for controls).

Asparagus beetles eat the spears and the foliage. They appear from early summer and are yellow and black and about 1cm (½in) long; their caterpillar-like larvae are grey-black. Both beetles and larvae are easily spotted and can be picked off by hand, as can the clusters of black eggs on foliage. Tidy up the browning asparagus ferns in autumn to discourage overwintering pests, and burn the cut foliage to kill any pests that still may be lurking.

Any sign of infestation is very off-putting on the plate. If you see blackfly while crops are growing, wipe them off developing buds with a damp cloth or a soft brush dipped in water.

HOW TO plant asparagus crowns

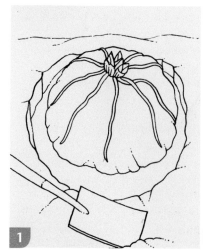

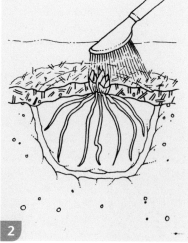

1 Prepare the soil well before planting – add organic matter the previous winter and then a fertilizer just beforehand. Dig a hole about 15cm (6in) deep and build a mound. Sit each crown on the top of the mound and arrange its roots down the slope as evenly as practical.

2 Ensuring that the crown will be slightly proud of the surface, and taking care not to dislodge it from its perch on top of the mound, backfill the hole with soil. Water it well, then cover the crown with about 8cm (3in) of soil and top it off with a generous mulch.

For the best flavour and texture, harvest asparagus spears before they get too long. You can use a sharp knife, but special serrated-edged asparagus knives are available.

Aubergines

SOW FEB, MAR **plant** MAY, JUN
harvest JUL, AUG, SEP, OCT

Aubergines are one of those vegetables that you try growing, have poor results with, and then don't bother with again. Think again – grow a couple of plants in pots in the warmest place in your garden, and given a good summer they might surprise you. If you raise plants from seed, you could try novelty varieties such as 'Calliope' (pink-striped) or 'Mohican' (white). These are decorative but the flavour is nothing special.

It is possible to get reasonable-sized fruit from aubergine plants. 'Moneymaker' is a good performer and suitable for outdoor cultivation, where it crops well in good summers.

Cultivation

DIFFICULTY Easy; low input but need the right conditions.
SOW at 21–24°C (70–75°F), in late winter/early spring. Prick out seedlings into small pots and grow on at 16–18°C (60–65°F) until late spring.
PLANT in a cold greenhouse in late spring. Alternatively, plant outside in early summer; but harden off first and wait for warm weather. Aubergine plants are often available at garden centres to save having to grow them from seed.
SPACE 60cm (2ft) apart in all directions.
CARE Water sparingly at first, increasing the supply as plants start carrying a crop, especially in hot weather. Feed weekly with liquid tomato feed once the first fruits have set. Support the main stems with canes (*see* page 56). Plants grow to about 90cm (3ft) high and 60cm (2ft) wide outdoors, slightly bigger under glass.
YIELD Up to 1.8kg (4lb) per plant – if you are lucky.
STORAGE Keep for a couple of weeks in the fridge.

Keep them happy by...

Growing them in a warm, sheltered place. Slow growth and low yields on poor plants are usually a sign that growing conditions are unsuitable: too cold, too wet or too windy.

Worth trying...

'Black Enorma' – Fat, purple-black aubergines, but only a few per plant. Slow to reach full size, so best in a greenhouse.
'Moneymaker' – Purple, sausage-shaped aubergines; reliable, high-yielder. Fruit are produced early, so a good choice for growing outdoors as they have a good chance of maturing.

Enjoy them...

From midsummer on, as soon as the fruit are 7.5cm (3in) long or more; use secateurs to cut the prickly stem 1cm (½in) beyond the fruit. Plants will continue to crop outside until cold nights strike in early autumn – crops grown under glass will continue for another month.

Look out for...

If fruit are left on the plants too long, they will taste bitter and develop small hard seeds. Harvest while still shiny.

Greenfly can stop the plants growing, especially early on and under glass. Remove small infestations by hand or use a suitable spray (*see* page 54).

Whitefly and red spider mite can be a problem. Use a biological control (*see* page 53).

Beans, broad

SOW LATE AUTUMN OR, FEB, MAR, APR
plant MAR, APR
harvest JUN, JUL

Broad beans are a favourite in traditional vegetable gardens. They are worth growing if you have the space for a reasonable number of plants, and are prepared to provide support: home-grown and fresh from the garden, they are far superior to any that you can buy, even those that are frozen within hours of picking. The flowers have a fabulous fragrance, too.

'The Sutton' is a long-standing favourite. Its dwarf stature makes it suitable for growing in smaller gardens.

Cultivation

DIFFICULTY Easy, but need regular care and attention.
SOW under cover in pots or trays in late winter and early spring, or outdoors in situ in mid-spring. Sow in succession in early and late spring and in late autumn for a longer season.
PLANT out indoor plants in mid-spring.
SPACE 20cm (8in) apart, in double rows 20cm (8in) apart, with 45cm (18in) between the double rows. If you have plenty of space, increase the double-row spacing to 60–90cm (2–3ft), which enables the plants to cope better with dry conditions and allows for easier weeding.
CARE Water routinely if the weather is dry. No extra feeding is needed throughout the growing season.
YIELD About 5.5kg (12lb) from a 2m (6ft) double row.
STORAGE If you have any to spare, freeze them (*see* Storage, pages 58–9) as soon as you pick them.

Keep them happy by...

Erecting some good support. Insert two 1.2m (4ft) posts at the end of each double row with two horizontal strings along each side of the double row of plants, at 30 and 60cm (12 and 24in) above the ground. As the plants grow the strings will hold them up without damaging the fragile stems.

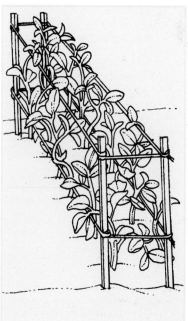

Support
Broad beans can make large leafy plants and they have weak stems, so it is important to provide strong supports. Do this when they are still small and easy to work with otherwise the job becomes much more difficult.

Worth trying…

'Aquadulce' – A tried-and-tested variety. Not a fantastic flavour, but the weatherproof plants are good from an early sowing and can also be sown in late autumn for an early spring crop.

'Imperial Green Longpod' – Bright green and tender beans in long pods on tall plants; a heavy cropper.

'Medes' – Short pods of tasty beans on mid-height plants. Only sow in spring.

'The Sutton' – Compact, 30cm (12in) tall, so needs less support. Can be sown in late autumn for an early crop in late spring; as it is short it is easy to protect early spring plants with cloches or gardener's fleece (see page 39).

Enjoy them…

Once the beans inside the pods are the size of a thumbnail – over a six-week period from early summer. Pick them by pulling back the pod against its direction of growth, then twisting slightly, or snip them with scissors or secateurs. After cropping, if you don't need the space for something else, cut the plants down to about 15cm (6in) or so above the ground – if you are lucky you may get a late smattering of beans towards the very end of summer.

Look out for…

Mice and pigeons regard broad bean seed as fair game and cold, wet, early-spring weather makes them rot; if your ground is less than well-drained, sow seed later in spring or raise your plants under cover.

The black bean aphid (blackfly) is a regular pest, congregating round the plant tips and on young pods. Once pods start to appear, nip out the plant's growing tips to remove their feeding sites.

Chocolate spot causes brown markings on the leaves. Avoid this fungus by feeding plants and providing good drainage and air circulation. Rust fungus produces red-brown markings on the leaves, but it occurs too late in the season to be a problem. Pea and bean weevil chew notches in the leaves – ugly, but this seldom affects yields.

If you want lots of broad beans, it is annoying that in some years seeds planted in autumn and then overwintered can be a complete failure!

Beans, French

Dwarf
SOW APR, MAY, JUN, JUL **plant** MAY
harvest JUN, JUL, AUG, SEP

Climbing
SOW APR, MAY, JUN **plant** MAY
harvest JUN, JUL, AUG

Flageolet, haricot
SOW APR, MAY, JUN **plant** MAY
harvest SEP, OCT

Green beans are near the top of the list of veg to grow. They don't take much space or time and they are fantastic fresh – much, much better than those jet-setting imports that have seen more of the world than you. If you become really keen, there is a wide range of types: connoisseur's, heritage, purple- or gold-podded, and those that can be dried. If you have a greenhouse you can also grow green beans 'out-of-season'.

'Blue Lake' has pencil-thin cylindrical pods and white seeds.

Cultivation

DIFFICULTY Easy, but need better growing conditions than runners; average input.

SOW on a warm windowsill indoors in mid-spring; outdoors in situ in late spring to midsummer – bear in mind that they are frost tender.

PLANT greenhouse-raised plants outdoors after the danger of frost is past in late spring.

SPACING Dwarf varieties 15cm (6in) apart with 25cm (10in) between rows; climbing varieties on supports 20cm (8in) apart.

CARE Water sparingly while they are young and in dull, cool weather, more generously after they are established and carrying a crop. No extra feeding is needed if the ground was well prepared before planting.

YIELD From a 1.5m (5ft) row – dwarf 1.8kg (4lb), climbing 2.7kg (6lb).

STORAGE Fine for a week in the fridge; can be frozen (*see* storage, pages 58–9).

Keep them happy by…

Avoiding planting them if the weather is cool, dull or damp – both the seeds and the young plants can rot. For early plants or if the summer is cold, plant seeds in small individual pots indoors and keep the seed compost on the dry side. Don't rush to put plants out until conditions are warmer and drier.

Worth trying…

'Blue Lake' – Climbing variety with cylindrical green pods. Large pods can be left to dry out for haricots.

'Cobra' – Climbing, heavy and long cropper with long, slender green pods and lilac flowers; attractive in a pot, and can be grown early under glass.

'Hunter' – Climbing, heavy cropper with large, flat (like runners), very tender, tasty pods for slicing. Grow in spring and late summer/autumn under glass as well as outdoors. Seeds can be difficult to obtain; 'Helda' is similar.

'Opera' – Dwarf, reliable heavy cropper with excellent flavour. Disease resistant, so good for organic growing.

'Purple Teepee' – Dwarf, heavy cropper with dark purple pods.

'Valdor' – Dwarf, heavy cropper; tasty pale gold pods. Long season and disease resistant.

Some for drying…

'Pea bean' – Old variety with small pods of pea-sized, cream beans with maroon spots. These can be shelled and used fresh

Special notes

OUT-OF-SEASON CROPS
Sow Dwarf French beans on a warm windowsill indoors in early spring. Plant them in the greenhouse in a well-prepared soil border, growing bags or large pots from mid-spring; avoid cold spells. Harvest in late spring and early summer. Sow in midsummer for plants to grow in an unheated greenhouse for cropping in early to mid-autumn.

FOR DRYING
Leave the pods to grow to full size and they'll start to turn yellow–brown as the beans ripen. Let them dry out naturally, if possible. If damp or frost threatens, pick them and finish the drying in shallow trays in a warm, dry place indoors. Shell the pods, spread out the beans to dry further, then store in jars.

or allowed to dry in the pods on the plants. Can be difficult to find. Keep some pods for next year's seed.

'Soissons' – Climbing bean with green seeds – flageolets when dry. Fine flavour.

Enjoy them…

As soon as the pods are big enough, so you can really appreciate them at their most tender. Pick them regularly otherwise the beans get too fat and coarse and are no longer good to eat. Dry out and save these beans for next year's seed.

Look out for…

Most beans really don't like cold wet conditions, avoid these and you will avoid most problems.

Even if you don't want haricots, it is tempting to grow 'Borlotto Lingua di Fuoco' just for the attractive maroon and white speckled pods. They make especially attractive climbing plants in the flower garden, where they provide height when grown up obelisks.

Beans, runner

SOW APR, MAY **plant** MAY, JUN
harvest JUL, AUG, SEP, OCT

The secret with runners is to eat them while small and tender; beans that have been left to grow huge become tough and stringy. Don't feel guilty about chucking them on the compost heap, as chances are they'll be plenty more young beans as these plants always produce bumper crops. If you think you hate runners, think again. Grow them yourself, don't grow too many, eat them young and you'll love them.

These healthy runner bean plants of the variety 'Lady Di' are just beginning to produce pods.

Cultivation

DIFFICULTY Easy; low input, apart from picking.
SOW in pots on a windowsill indoors in mid-spring, or outdoors in situ in late spring.
PLANT out pot-grown specimens in early summer.
SPACE 23cm (9in) apart in rows or on wigwams.
CARE Water thoroughly in dry spells. Also spray the plants daily to increase humidity. In very dry weather, give the plants a thorough soaking then mulch them with garden compost or old newspapers. Never let the soil dry out completely. Extra feeding isn't needed for plants in well-prepared patches; for those in containers or intensive veg beds, apply liquid tomato feed weekly while plants are carrying crops.
YIELD A dozen plants will feed a family of four and allow some beans to be frozen.
STORAGE Put them in the fridge for up to a week if you must; can be frozen (*see* Storage, pages 58–9).

Keep them happy by…

Providing tall supports – canes need to be 2.5m (8ft) tall; 30cm (12in) of which needs to be pushed into the ground. Spray open flowers with water to encourage 'setting'. Never let the soil dry out completely. Yes, I know I've said that already, but it's important!

Worth trying…

'Enorma' – Very long, straight pods; tender and tasty.
'Lady Di' – Long, slender, flavoursome, stringless beans; seedless until quite well developed with a long growing season.
'Sunset' – Shortish beans with a good flavour early in the season. Pale pink flowers make this ideal for a pot or even a flower garden.
'White Swan' – A heavy cropper producing long and wide beans over a long period; white-flowered.

Enjoy them…

As soon as they are upwards of 10cm (4in) long. When they are growing quickly, many large-podded varieties are still good at 30–38cm (12–15in). Once they have developed seeds they aren't worth eating.

Look out for…

Birds may peck off the flowers and snails enjoy high-rise living on the supports and are partial to the occasional pod, as well as the leaves. Flower drop may occur in dry weather.

Beetroot

SOW MAR, APR, MAY, JUN
harvest JUL, AUG, SEP, OCT

Fresh beetroot is wonderful roasted or boiled, or even grated raw; and the leaves can be used young in salads. When home-grown and picked while still small, beetroot is sweet and full of flavour – you'll never be able to face the pickled variety again. The natural, vivid purple colour of beetroot is caused by anti-oxidants, which, it is claimed, are good for your health.

Smallish roots from an early harvest of 'Boltardy'. A tried-and-tested favourite with a good flavour, this variety is less likely to bolt than some other beetroots.

Cultivation

DIFFICULTY Intermediate; average input.

SOW early bolt-resistant varieties in early spring; other varieties from mid-spring to midsummer. For a really early crop, sow a few seeds in a greenhouse border in late winter.

SPACE Sow 'seed' 2.5cm (1in) apart in rows; thin seedlings to 7.5cm (3in) apart for babies, or 15cm (6in) apart for full-sized roots. (The 'seed' are capsules containing several seeds.)

CARE Water during dry spells to keep plants growing steadily; no extra feeding is needed. Weed to prevent young plants from being swamped.

YIELD About 2.3kg (5lb) from a 1.5m (5ft) row.

STORAGE Keep in the fridge for up to two weeks.

Keep them happy by...

Protecting plants with fleece in cold weather.

Worth trying...

'Albina Vereduna' – White globes with a sweet flavour.

'Boltardy' – Bolt-resistant, traditional roots with a good taste and texture.

'Burpee's Golden' – Globe-shaped, golden roots; superb flavour. Good for picking small.

'Cylindra' – Tall, tubular roots form above ground, up to 20cm (8in) tall; produces a huge crop from a single row; no good for baby beet.

'Detroit 6-Rubidus' – Reliable, bolt-resistant globes for early crops. Doesn't get woody, even when allowed to grow large.

Enjoy them...

As early as late spring, as baby beetroot around 2.5cm (1in) in diameter. Pull every third or fourth plant, leaving the rest with space to continue growing. Use full-sized roots as needed during summer. Roots tend to store best in the ground; lift the remainder in mid-autumn, keep under cover in a cool place to use as soon as possible.

Look out for...

Beetroot is very prone to bolting (running to seed) if sown too early or when growing conditions are difficult for them (*see* Keep them happy by...). Use varieties bred for early sowing if you suffer regular bolting. Water more regularly if your roots turn out woody.

Broccoli, sprouting

SOW APR, MAY plant JUN, JUL
harvest JAN, FEB, MAR

Sprouting broccoli is incredibly tasty and a very reliable winter crop, not to be confused with the summer-cropping calabrese (see page 76). The sprouting spears are amazingly tender for plants that grow through winter and this is one of those vegetables that is unbeatable picked and cooked within minutes. Just a few plants are enough for a real treat with hearty winter meals.

Purple sprouting broccoli in summer

'Bordeaux' and 'Summer Purple' are summer croppers, although their season is brief. Sow seeds under cover from late winter and at three-week intervals until early summer, plant out from mid-spring and have crops from midsummer. Combine these varieties with the winter ones and you could have tender shoots of sprouting broccoli all year round.

Cultivation

DIFFICULTY Easy, low input.

SOW from mid-spring/late spring in a seedbed; thin to 7.5–10cm (3–4in) apart.

PLANT out the young plants from the seedbed to the main bed in early to midsummer.

SPACE 45cm (18in) apart in each direction.

CARE Plant in very firm ground and water in dry spells. Give a general-purpose liquid feed in late summer, or use a granular feed with plenty of water to wash it in.

YIELD About 600g (1½lb) per plant.

STORAGE Keeps for up to three days in the fridge.

Keep them happy by...

Supporting plants in exposed sites. Tie main stems to stakes before the autumn winds start picking up.

Worth trying...

'Claret' – Very late – for picking in mid-spring; purple spears.
'Late Purple Sprouting' – Crops in early to mid-spring.
'Rudolph' – Very early, purple spears, ready from early to late winter; large, tasty shoots.
'White Sprouting' – Crops in early spring; green-white spears.

Enjoy them...

As soon as the colour of the developing heads is visible, cut the entire shoot 5–10cm (2–4in) long with a sharp knife. Check plants at least twice a week and don't allow any shoots to run to seed; the more you cut, the more will grow, but once they flower, they stop producing new shoots.

Look out for...

In fact, most varieties of sprouting broccoli are amazingly pest free, since the edible part forms in late winter or early spring when there are no cabbage white butterflies about. Summer varieties of purple sprouting broccoli (see left) may be more prone; if they strike, pick them off (see page 55).

Clubroot can ruin crops and prevent you from growing brassicas for years (see page 74). Pigeons can be a problem: cover brassicas with fine-mesh netting or bird netting (see page 52).

This plant of 'Late Purple Sprouting' broccoli should have a long cropping season and is a handsome addition to a flower border.

Brussels sprouts

SOW FEB, MAR, APR **plant** MAY, JUN
harvest JAN, FEB, MAR AND SEP, OCT, NOV, DEC

What a surprise that sprouts have turned out to be good for you! They contain anti-oxidants, which are thought to help fight cancer. These slightly peppery mini cabbages are not to everyone's liking, but in common with so many vegetables, the home-produced ones are far superior to anything you can buy.

Sprouts are great winter vegetables whose flavour is improved by exposure to frost. They are available for harvesting throughout the autumn and winter.

Cultivation

DIFFICULTY Easy; lowish input.

SOW at 13–16°C (55–60°F) indoors in late winter and early spring for early croppers, or in an outdoor seedbed in early spring and mid-spring for later ones.

PLANT out indoor-raised seedlings in late spring after careful hardening off. Those plants started off in seedbeds can be planted in situ in early summer.

SPACE 60cm (2ft) apart in all directions, further apart (75cm/2½ft) where there is more room.

CARE Water well in dry spells. Give a boost in the form of a general-purpose fertilizer in late summer and water in.

YIELD Around 1kg (2¼lb) per plant.

STORAGE Keep for a few days in the fridge; can be frozen (*see* Storage, pages 58–9).

Keep them happy by…

Making sure the soil is very firm; tread it down well before and after planting, using your heel around the plants. Stake in exposed sites.

Worth trying…

'Darkmar' – Heavy cropper with dark green sprouts from late autumn.

'Falstaff' – Mild, reddish purple buttons from mid-autumn to early winter.

'Trafalgar' – Sweetish sprouts produced in heavy crops from early winter to early spring; tall plants.

Enjoy them…

As soon as they are large enough to eat – from the size of a large marble. Cropping from early varieties begins in early autumn, later ones from late autumn; the latest can be picked up until early spring.

Look out for…

Pigeons, which target the young plants: use protection (*see* page 52). Instead of forming tight buttons, sprouts sometimes 'blow' – they open out into small, flattened, green rosettes. Avoid growing them in loose soil and stake them if in doubt. Clubroot is a threat (*see* page 74).

Cabbages

Summer- and autumn-hearting and red
SOW MAR, APR **plant** MAY, JUN
harvest AUG, SEP, OCT

Winter-hearting and Savoy
SOW APR, MAY **plant** JUN
harvest JAN, FEB AND NOV, DEC

Spring-hearting
SOW JUL, AUG **plant** SEP, OCT
harvest APR, MAY

The name 'cabbage' encompasses a treasure trove of vegetables in a range of colours (white, green, red) and textures (smooth, crispy, deeply wrinkled). They are tasty, healthy and versatile. If you haven't yet tasted coleslaw made with your own home-grown cabbages, then make this the year that you do.

Cultivation

DIFFICULTY Intermediate; it is worth a little extra care.
SOW early varieties under cover and later types in a seedbed, thinning out the latter and transplanting them as appropriate.
PLANT out summer and autumn cabbages, including red cabbage, in late spring and early summer; winter cabbage and Savoys in midsummer; spring cabbage in mid-autumn.
SPACE Depends on the variety: allow 30cm (12in) apart for smaller ones, bigger ones need 45cm (18in). Increase spacing if you have more room.
CARE Keep watered in dry spells so that plants can grow continuously without a check. Apply a top-up general-purpose or high-nitrogen feed during the summer to encourage leafy growth; water in well.
YIELD Varies according to variety.
STORAGE Cabbages are best left attached to their stems in the ground until you want to eat them.

Clubroot

Clubroot is a problem with brassicas. It is easily brought in on young plants raised in infected ground elsewhere. The roots of plants such as cabbages, broccoli and Brussels sprouts swell and eventually rot, and the top growth is badly stunted. Once you have clubroot it stays in the ground for 20 years or more, during which time you can't grow any members of the cabbage family (it also affects flowering members of the family) – there's no 'cure'. Make sure you don't get it by raising all your own plants, by growing brassicas in well-drained soil and by liming acid soil prior to planting. The disease is less common on chalky, alkaline soils and where drainage is good (*see* pages 27–30).

It's not surprising that cabbages are popular in decorative potagers. This is the Savoy variety 'January King', which looks especially decorative when covered with frost.

Keep them happy by...

Planting them in well-prepared firm ground, weeding regularly, and taking care not to disturb their shallow roots.

Worth trying...

There are numerous cabbage varieties, so you might want to experiment. Here are some good ones:

'Cuor di Bue' (Bull's heart) – A full-flavoured winter cabbage with tight conical heads in late summer and autumn. The seeds can be hard to obtain – try the Internet.

'Golden Acre' – Summer-hearting, ball-headed cabbage; sow in late winter.

'Hispi' – Summer- and autumn-hearting; the one to choose if you grow no others. Tasty and fast growing with small hearts. Sow from late winter under cover and from early spring to midsummer outdoors. Sow under cover in mid-autumn and raise the plants in a unheated greenhouse border for cutting early in spring. 'Hispi' is also suitable as 'baby' veg: plant 23cm (9in) apart in each direction.

'January King' – Savoy cabbage tinged with red; matures in autumn and can be left in place through winter from a late-spring sowing.

'Kalibos' – Heirloom red variety with pointed heads.

'Red Jewel' – Good round-headed, red-leaved variety.

'Wheeler's Imperial' – Compact spring cabbage. Sow in summer for a spring harvest or late winter for an autumn crop.

'Winter King' – Savoy with crumpled leaves. Several sowings in late spring and early summer will stagger the crop, extending your Savoy season into late winter.

Enjoy them...

When the centre tightens up and forms a solid 'heart'. Use secateurs or a knife with a scalloped blade to cut through the stem just below the heart. Remove damaged outer leaves. Leave the rest on to protect the interior. With careful planning you should have cabbage varieties all year round.

Look out for...

Cabbage white butterflies (large and small) love brassicas, and their caterpillars eat the leaves and deposit frass (excrement), making them unfit to eat. Cover growing crops (*see* page 52). Remove caterpillars by hand or use an organic pesticide.

Small slugs can work their way into the hearts of developing cabbages, causing damage and leaving droppings. For slug controls *see* page 54.

Pigeons like cabbages as winter forage – put bird netting in place if necessary to keep them off the crop (*see* page 52).

Cabbage root fly lays its eggs at the base of the stem and the larvae eat the roots, causing the plant to wilt and die. Buy small collars made from roofing-felt (specifically made for protecting crops) and slip these around the base of each stem to prevent egg laying. Fine mesh properly fitted above and around the plants also helps (*see* page 52). Clubroot can occur, *see* box.

The hearts of 'Hispi' develop in summer and autumn, making neat conical heads of fresh green leaves.

Calabrese (green broccoli)

SOW MAR, APR, MAY **plant** APR, MAY, JUN
harvest JUN, JUL, AUG, SEPT

Calabrese is a delicious and deservedly popular vegetable. It is similar to broccoli (and often known as such) but with solid cauliflower-like heads. If you cut the central head and leave the plants in the ground, you get some smaller 'spears' a few weeks later – which makes it a good-value crop into the bargain. It's also easily grown, especially in polytunnels.

Cultivation

DIFFICULTY Intermediate; needs regular care.

SOW under cover in early spring, or in an outside seedbed from mid-spring. In a polytunnel, sow in succession (about every six weeks) all year round apart from midwinter.

PLANT outdoors in late spring or early summer.

SPACE 30cm (12in) apart in each direction.

CARE It is vital to keep the plant growing steadily, so water and weed regularly and use a boost of general-purpose or high-nitrogen feed halfway through the growing season.

YIELD About 600g (1½lb) per plant.

STORAGE The heads will keep for a few days in the fridge if picked with a length of stalk.

Keep them happy by...

Protecting them from caterpillars (*see* page 54). They are very popular with cabbage whites, which will get to them anywhere (even in a polytunnel) if they are not covered with a fine-mesh netting (make sure that the netting does not touch the leaves).

Worth trying...

'Crown and Sceptre' – A large central head in summer is followed by several pickings of smaller spears in late summer and autumn.

'Chevalier' – Medium-sized heads are followed by small spears from early autumn onwards.

'Kabuki' – Compact plants that mature early for baby calabrese; grow closer together.

Enjoy them...

From early summer into autumn. Cut off the whole head and use as required.

Look out for...

They suffer the same problems as all the cabbage family, including clubroot (*see* page 74).

Although calabrese is available all year round at the greengrocers and in the supermarket, there's nothing to match the flavour of home-grown varieties, such as 'Chevalier'.

Carrots Early varieties

SOW MAR AND JUL, AUG
harvest JUN, JUL AND OCT, NOV

Carrots are fantastic eaten young, either raw or lightly steamed. When you grow your own you can experiment with all the different coloured (and shaped) varieties, which are not available in the shops. Maincrop carrots (see box) are best for real carrot enthusiasts and those who want to eat everything organic, as the organic type are expensive to buy.

Cultivation

DIFFICULTY Intermediate; pay attention and give regular care.
SOW thinly in shallow seed drills. Sow early varieties under cloches or fleece in early spring, then again in midsummer and late summer for a few quick, late pickings; cover these with fleece in the autumn to extend the growing season.
SPACE Sow as thinly as you can as thinning carrots releases an aroma that attracts carrot fly. Allow 30cm (12in) between rows.

The smooth-skinned carrot variety 'Yellowstone' produces sweet roots at their best eaten raw. You'll find that home-grown carrots are markedly sweeter than those bought in the shops, especially if they are cooked within minutes of being harvested.

CARE Water well during dry spells and weed regularly to keep the roots growing steadily. Take precautions against carrot fly; avoid thinning out seedlings as the scent may draw carrot flies to your crop which could ruin it (*see* pages 52–3).
YIELD Around 2kg (4½lb) from a 1.5m (5ft) row.
STORAGE Pull and eat early varieties. If necessary, store them in a paper sack in a cool place. Check them regularly and eat as soon as possible.

Keep them happy by...

Cultivating the soil until it is fine textured without lumps or stones before sowing seed – and don't put them in ground that has been manured in the last 12 months.

Worth trying...

'Autumn King' – Large, tapering carrots; ready in autumn but keep well in well-drained ground over winter.
'Healthmaster' – Deep red-orange carrots with increased beta-carotene; use raw for the best nutritional benefits.
'Nantes' – Sweet-tasting long roots ready in early summer from a protected late winter sowing. 'Nantes' can also be sown at the same time as other earlies. Improved forms, such as 'Nantes 2', are identical.
'Samurai' – Red-skinned carrots with pink flesh that retains its colour even when cooked. Ready in summer and autumn.
'Sugarsnax' – Long thin carrots for eating raw.
'Yellowstone' – Sweet, bright yellow carrots; best in salads.

Enjoy them...

As baby or salad carrots as soon as the first ones are big enough to use, leaving the rest to keep growing (around midsummer). Pull alternate carrots to give those left behind more room to grow (carrot flies are less trouble later in the season).

Maincrop varieties

If you want to grow maincrop carrot varieties, sow carrot seed in the open in mid- and late spring and early summer when the soil has had a chance to warm up. You can leave the crop in the ground, until rainy weather starts in autumn. After this they are liable to produce fine, white root hairs and resprout, so dig them up, brush them off and let them dry. Washing them encourages rot.

Look out for...

Carrot fly is almost inevitable. The best solution is to keep carrots covered with fine, insect-proof mesh throughout their lives. Grow rows of onions and spring onions around them to disguise the scent that attracts carrot flies.

There are nearly always one or two fanged roots. If your whole crop is badly affected, you have probably added too much organic matter to the veg bed too recently. Stony soil can produce the same effect though. If necessary, make a raised bed (*see* pages 18–20) and fill it with sieved soil mixed with old potting compost to give the carrots a good root run.

Beat the flies

There are several carrot-fly resistant varieties such as 'Flyway', 'Maestro' and 'Resistafly'. However, they often prove to be less tasty than other 'non-resistant' varieties and are not 100 per cent effective: small outbreaks of carrot fly may still occur.

Where carrot flies are a problem, try growing onions in among your carrots. Members of the onion family (alliums) are thought to discourage this pest.

Cauliflowers

Summer-heading cauliflowers
SOW JAN, FEB plant MAR, APR
harvest MAY, JUN, JUL

Autumn-heading cauliflowers
SOW MAR plant APR MAY
harvest AUG, SEP, OCT, NOV

Winter-heading cauliflowers
SOW APR, MAY plant MAY, JUN
harvest FEB, MAR, APR

Cauliflowers have undergone a change: aside from the traditional white type, which we are all familiar with, you can now get a rainbow of colours – well, green, yellow-green and purple anyway. These look pretty, although for flavour and texture you can't beat the white ones. On the downside, cauliflowers aren't a breeze to grow, but if you have space, try a few.

Cultivation

DIFFICULTY Advanced; look after well. Not time consuming.
SOW summer varieties indoors at 16°C (60°F); autumn varieties indoors or in a seedbed under cover (such as a coldframe, greenhouse border or under fleece outdoors) and winter varieties in a seedbed outdoors.
PLANT out young plants at 7.5–10cm (3–4in) tall with a good root system.
SPACE 60cm (2ft) apart for summer and autumn varieties; 75cm (2½ft) for winter varieties.
CARE Keep plants well weeded and watered through the summer. Boost the plants with a general-purpose or high-nitrogen feed around mid- to late summer.
YIELD If you are lucky, up to 1kg (2.2lb) per plant, but probably considerably less.
STORAGE Wrap in clingfilm and store in a fridge for up to a week; can be frozen as florets (*see* Storage, pages 58–9).

Keep them happy by...

Really excelling at your soil preparation; as with all brassicas, firm soil is essential.

Bend a few outer leaves over the cauliflower head as the curds bulk up (snap the leaf midrib to keep it in place). This is especially important for white varieties, which easily discolour.

Worth trying…

'All Year Round' – Traditional white cauliflowers, all seasons from successional sowings. Sow in mid-autumn and protect the plants in a polytunnel or under fleece for spring crops.

'Autumn Giant' – Reliable autumn-header, firm white curds.

'Clapton' – An autumn-header with long leaves that protect the developing heads; resistant to clubroot.

'Purple Cape' – Good variety with tasty, large, deep purple heads that keep their colour reasonably well on cooking. Takes nearly a year to grow, but the result is well worth it.

'Romanesco' – Lime-green curds form a series of pinnacles instead of a smooth flat head; good for dividing into florets for salads or steaming; keeps its colour when cooked. Ready in late summer/autumn. 'Celio' and 'Veronica' are similar.

'Trevi' – Bright green heads with a wonderful flavour; keeps its colour on cooking. Sow in late spring, eat in early autumn.

'Violet Queen' – Mauve heads ready in late summer/early autumn; turns green when cooked.

Baby cauliflowers

Mini-cauliflowers – one-per-person-size – are great fresh and for freezing. You need to buy specially bred 'baby veg' or 'patio variety' seeds. The range increases each year, but 'Igloo' and 'Avalanche' are good. Plant them closer together than normal – approx 30–45cm (12–18in) apart.

Enjoy them…

Once the developing curds form a dense, tightly packed hemisphere; cut it off just beneath the base of the head (include the collar of outer leaves as these will provide protection until you use the cauliflower). Pick as soon as the head is level all over; don't delay, as the florets soon start to shoot out individually and quickly open into flowers.

Look out for…

Cauliflowers suffer the same problems as cabbages, including clubroot (*see* page 74).

Unfavourable weather can produce small or ruined heads. If it's the weather, this is unavoidable, but inadequate soil preparation can also be a factor.

'All Year Round' is a traditional-style cauliflower with large white curds.

The cauliflower variety 'Romanesco' has vivid green heads with pointed curds.

Celeriac

SOW MAR **plant** MAY, JUN
harvest JAN, FEB, MAR AND SEP, OCT, NOV, DEC

With it's lumpy misshapen roots that grow half out of the ground, no-one could call celeriac an attractive vegetable, but it certainly is tasty, and it's much easier to grow than its refined relative, celery. It is one of those veg that are pricey in the shops, so it's worth your while trying to grow a few.

Cultivation

DIFFICULTY Intermediate; pay attention to detail.
SOW in early spring on a windowsill indoors at 16–21°C (60–70°F). Prick out seedlings into small pots and continue growing in warmth (13°C/55°F minimum) on a windowsill or in a heated propagator in a greenhouse. Keep well watered and in good light, but not strong sun.
PLANT into soil containing plenty of well-rotted organic matter after hardening off and when the last frost is safely past (late spring onwards).
SPACE Minimum 30cm (12in) apart in all directions if you are restricted for space; 45cm (18in) apart if you can.
CARE Administer general-purpose liquid feed as often as every two weeks and keep plants well watered at all times. Weed regularly until plants are big enough to cover the ground and shade out weeds naturally.
YIELD A row of 1.5m (5ft) gives about 1.5kg (3½lb).
STORAGE Dig them up as you need them; keeps for a few days in the fridge.

Worth trying…

'Monarch' – A reliable variety with good-quality roots.

Keep them happy by…

Preparing the soil well: rich soil is the key to succulent roots. They hate poor, dry earth. Don't stint on food and water as the plants need to be able to grow steadily.

Enjoy them…

From early autumn, as soon as the first roots are big enough. Dig up the whole plant, rest it on a hard surface and slice off the top, including all the leaves. Remove the smaller roots. You will need a strong knife.

In mild winters you can have celeriac until early spring. Leave them in the ground until you want them.

Look out for…

Celery fly (*see* page 81) may cause problems, otherwise crop failure is usually due to cultivation deficiencies or adverse weather. However, even imperfect roots are fine for making soups.

What it lacks in beauty celeriac makes up for in flavour, but it needs really rich soil to put on weight.

Celery (self-blanching)

SOW MAR plant MAY, JUN
harvest AUG, SEP, OCT

Celery is delicious to eat raw and also imparts a
wonderful rich flavour to a wide variety of stews, soups
and other concoctions in the kitchen. However, it must
be well aware of its value because it is very demanding
in the vegetable garden and one of the most difficult
crops to grow successfully.

Celery plants require perfect growing conditions to do well.

Cultivation

DIFFICULTY Advanced; challenging and time consuming.
SOW on a windowsill indoors at 16–21°C (60–70°F) in early
spring. Prick out seedlings into small pots as soon as they are
large enough to handle, and continue growing in warmth
(13°C/55°F minimum) on a windowsill or in a heated
propagator in a greenhouse. Keep the plants well watered and
in adequate light, but not strong sun. Harden off carefully.
PLANT out when the last frost is past – from early summer.
SPACE 23cm (9in) apart in all directions. Close spacing ensures
the plants shade each others' stems, which helps them to
blanch. Grow them in blocks, with an edging of raised boards
to prevent the stems of the plants at the edges being turned
green by the light.
CARE Keep plants well watered at all times – they must never
go even slightly short of moisture. Give a liquid feed regularly
from planting time onwards, using a general-purpose or
high-nitrogen fertilizer. Keep well weeded until plants cover
the ground enough to shade out weeds for themselves.
YIELD Depends how successful you are.
STORAGE Although it will keep in a fridge for a few days, why
not eat it while it's fresh?

Keep them happy by…

Providing them with rich fertile soil that contains quantities of
well-rotted organic matter. Celery hates a struggle – keep the
plants growing by watering and feeding assiduously.

Worth trying…

'Victoria' – A self-blanching F1 hybrid; the easiest to
grow successfully.

Enjoy them…

When the sticks are an edible size – this will be late summer. Self-
blanching celery isn't hardy, so use it before the first proper frost.

Look out for…

Slugs can get in between the stems and eat the plant centres,
which will then fall prey to bacterial infections and rots. Take
strict precautions against slugs at all times, starting several
weeks before planting.

Celery fly can be a nuisance, mining the leaves and leaving
blotches and ribbon-shaped tunnels. Pinch off and destroy any
badly infected leaves.

Carrot fly may also attack (see page 78).

Chicory

SOW JUN, JUL
harvest OCT, NOV, DEC

Chicory is one of those vegetables that some people like and some hate. It is slightly bitter tasting and forms heads rather like a lettuce, which can be cooked or used in salads. Witloof varieties are usually forced, which means they are grown without light to keep the leaves tightly furled, pale and tender. Other types, of which radicchio is one (it may be sold under 'R' in seed catalogues), are grown 'normally' for salad leaves.

Cultivation

DIFFICULTY Fairly easy; forcing varieties (see box) need time and effort.
SOW In situ – thin the seedlings, but don't transplant them.
SPACE 30cm (12in) apart in all directions.
CARE Water in dry spells, and keep well weeded.
YIELD A 1.5m (5ft) row gives about 1.25kg (2¾lb).
STORAGE Remains fresh in the fridge for a week or two.

Keep them happy by…

Giving them a long growing season and ensuring conditions are as good as possible. Radicchio can be temperamental but 'Sugar Loaf' should be pretty reliable. If all else fails, it can be forced as well (*see* box).

Forcing chicory

'Witloof Zoom' is the standard forcing variety. Grow the plants as usual and in late autumn cut down the tops to 7–8cm (3in) above the ground, dig up the roots and store them in slightly damp buckets of sand or soil in a cool shed.

Forcing takes 3–4 weeks. Depending on how much chicory you eat, force 3–4 roots at a time. Plant the roots in pots of moist compost, so their tops are just below the surface, then put them in a warm, dark place. Check regularly and water lightly if necessary – don't overdo it.

When the emerging buds are 7.5–10cm (3–4in) tall, cut them off at the base to use – don't wait, as they soon start to open and spoil. The same roots should produce several more 'chicons' before they need replacing with a new batch of roots from the shed.

Worth trying…

'Rossa di Verona' – Tightly packed leaves form mahogany-red radicchio hearts. Non-forcing.
'Sugar Loaf' – Upright, green-hearted non-forcing chicory with substantial inner leaves. Very reliable; good in polytunnels, where it can be left for some time in winter without rotting or bolting.

Enjoy them…

When they have formed hearts from mid-autumn onwards. Leave slowcoaches as they may heart up anytime until mid-spring. Forcing chicory should provide you with fare from midwinter.

Look out for…

Red varieties can stay green. Red radicchio only changes colour towards autumn, when the nights start growing cold. If it is green but has hearted up, you can still eat it.

Slugs and snails are less of a problem than they are with lettuce, they must dislike the bitter taste.

Pale and interesting – forced 'Witloof Zoom' chicory at the point of perfection and ready for harvesting.

Chillies

SOW FEB, MAR plant MAY, JUN
harvest JUL, AUG, SEP, OCT

Chillies are very fashionable and come in a wide range of shapes, colours and 'heats': if you don't want your tongue set on fire, there are plenty of mild ones that add a pleasant zing to a meal. The plants are attractive too, and some varieties can crop quite well on a sheltered patio, though growing them under cover gives more assured results.

Cultivation

DIFFICULTY Relatively easy; low input.

SOW in pots or trays at 21–24°C (70–75°F).

PLANT in early spring by first pricking out the seedlings into 7.5cm (3in) pots. Grow them on in an unheated greenhouse from late spring; or wait a month and for some settled warm weather before putting them outside.

SPACE One or two plants of each variety should have you overflowing with chillies, but if you grow more allow 30cm (12in) between compact varieties, 45cm (18in) between normal varieties and 60cm (2ft) between rows.

CARE Water sparingly, especially in cool conditions and while the plants are small. Feed weekly with liquid tomato feed. The stems are brittle so provide support. No pruning or trimming is needed.

YIELD Some plants produce loads of tiny fruits, others only a few big ones.

STORAGE Use fresh as required or dry them and put them in clean dry jars – whole or ground up.

Keep them happy by…

Plant them in a sheltered protected spot. A cold, dull or windy site or a poor summer can spell disaster.

Worth trying…

'Apache' – Compact plants; ideal for pots and on windowsills; green/red mid-strength fruits.

'Jalapeño' – Short, mid-strength green/red chillies with a slightly cracked skin.

'Joe's Long Cayenne' – Huge cropper; very long (to 30cm/10in) slim chillies, ripening red with a rich, fairly mild flavour.

'Mustard Habanero' – Very hot chillies with an unusual shape and colour – cream to purple to orange. Best under cover.

'Jalapeño' chillies used to be the most famous, but they've been overtaken by hotter ones with more exotic names; they're still among the best for general use, though.

'Thai Dragon' – Large crops of slender, achingly hot, green then red fruits.

Enjoy them…

Green as soon as they are large enough to use (usually from midsummer), or leave them to reach full size and turn red and develop their full flavour. Snip off a whole chilli plus part of its short green stalk.

Move container-grown plants under cover in autumn to extend the season, or pull up the plant, hang it upside down in a shed or not-too-hot kitchen to continue ripening, and let the chillies dry out naturally on the plant.

Look out for…

Greenfly like the plants too. They are mostly seen early on. Wipe them off by hand or use an organic spray as soon as you see them.

Courgettes, marrows, summer squashes

SOW APR **plant** MAY, JUN
harvest JUN, JUL, AUG, SEP, OCT

Once you have eaten a home-grown courgette you'll never want the thin-skinned, watery-flavoured, shop-sold ones again. Courgette plants are prolific – you'll only need one or two to have more than enough to eat. Marrows, which are more-or-less courgettes that have reached maturity, are good for stuffing and baking. Summer squashes can be grown and used just like courgettes – they only differ in shape.

Cultivation

DIFFICULTY Easy; low input.
SOW singly in small pots indoors from mid-spring.
PLANT young plants out from early summer after the last frosts. Harden them off first.
SPACE 60cm (2ft) apart in each direction for compact varieties, otherwise 90cm–1.2m (3–4ft) apart.
CARE Water young plants carefully, increasing the quantity as they grow. Ideally, apply liquid tomato feed every week while plants are carrying a crop.
YIELD More than you need from two or three plants.
STORAGE Best eaten fresh, but will keep in a fridge for a week.

Keep them happy by...

Giving them rich, fertile soil with plenty of organic matter – the more the better; you can even grow them on the compost heap. Don't plant them out too soon as they aren't hardy and you won't gain anything. They grow very rapidly once conditions are right. If fruits fail to develop it is almost always due to cool weather. Hand pollination can help. The failure of female flowers to appear is usually also due to cold weather.

Worth trying...

'Clarion' – Pale green courgettes with a very mild flavour; good for using raw.
'Defender' – An early, heavy-cropper producing dark green courgettes; resistant to the virus that can ruin courgette crops.
'Orelia' – Long yellow courgettes on a vigorous plant.
'Parthenon' – A compact parthenocarpic courgette with dark green fruits which sets without being pollinated.
'Patty Pan' – A summer squash with tasty, flying-saucer-shaped, pale green fruits.
'Sunburst' – Similar to 'Patty Pan' but with golden fruits.
'Tiger Cross' – A compact, heavy-cropping and virus-resistant bush marrow, producing large crops of tender light-and-dark green striped marrows.
See also page 109: Squashes and pumpkins.

For a good all-round, tasty traditional courgette, it is hard to beat 'Defender'.

Enjoy them…

As soon as they are big enough to use; courgettes from 10cm (4in), summer squashes from golf-ball size. Leave marrows until they are bigger (15–25cm/6–10in long). There's no need to wait until the flower has fallen off the end of the fruit. Cut through the stalk with a sharp knife. Avoid cutting into the plant or other fruit – it's easily done. Remove any rotting, misshapen or damaged courgettes at the same time, and discard. Plants will continue to crop until mid-autumn.

Look out for…

Cucumber mosaic virus can affect plants, as yellow-flecks at first, then the leaves turn increasingly yellow-patterned and crinkled and plants become stunted and unproductive. The disease is spread by aphids and by knives used for cutting crops. Choose resistant varieties where possible; many garden plants carry the disease so it is difficult to avoid. Pull out and dispose of affected plants.

Young plants that fail to thrive are often found to have virtually no roots when they are dug up. This is usually due to poor growing conditions and/or over-watering, but it may sometimes be harmful organisms in the manure or garden compost. To be on the safe side, start again with new plants in another spot.

Powdery mildew, a grey-white talcum-powder-like deposit on the foliage, often appears as nights start turning cool in the autumn, especially after a dry summer. Plants usually continue cropping lightly. Improve vigour by liquid feeding and watering generously; remove the worst affected leaves by hand.

'Patty Pan' squashes are shown here with a harvest of green marrows and yellow courgettes. Lightly steam these small squashes for a hot crunchy treat.

Extend the season

You can plant courgette seeds up to a month earlier in a greenhouse or polytunnel as long as you protect them with gardener's fleece on cold nights. However, protecting them in this way does mean that pollinating insects are less likely to reach them. To solve this problem, choose a variety that produces fruit without pollination (parthenocarpic). Also, try planting some courgettes under cover in late summer; these will provide fruit until the cold nights of autumn.

Large crops of light-and-dark green striped marrows are best cut and stored in a cool place. Do not leave them lying on the soil or their skins will deteriorate.

Cucumbers

Greenhouse
sow APR **plant** MAY
harvest JUL, AUG, SEP, OCT

Outdoor
sow APR **plant** MAY, JUN
harvest JUL, AUG, SEP

There is nothing quite like cutting your own fresh cucumbers and eating them while still standing out in the garden. They are crunchy, tasty and very moreish. It will make you wonder how those that are sold in the supermarkets got past the Trades Descriptions Act. There is little to choose between indoor and outdoor cucumbers for taste, but indoor ones are likely to have the edge on production, as they are less subject to the vagaries of the weather.

Indoors or out, 'Crystal Lemon' tends to produce more cucumbers than you dreamed you would need. It is best peeled as the skin can be tough and spiky.

Cultivation

DIFFICULTY Intermediate; won't stand neglect.
SOW seeds singly in small pots indoors – in mid-spring for greenhouse plants, late spring for outdoor plants.
PLANT on into a greenhouse in late spring, or outdoors from early summer, after hardening off the seedlings.
SPACE 45cm (18in) apart; one or two plants should suffice.
CARE Water sparingly at first and increase gradually as they come into full growth – when cropping, cucumbers need large amounts of water during hot weather. Feed regularly with general-purpose liquid feed. Cucumbers need support. To support: tie the main stem of indoor plants to a vertical bamboo cane, adding ties as the plant grows; outdoor plants need a wigwam, netting or other firm support (*see* Protection and Support, pages 56–7). For good-sized fruit you should also prune them. To prune: remove all sideshoots from the bottom 60cm (2ft) of the plant; allow higher sideshoots to develop. By the time each of these has grown about 15–20cm (6–8in) long, they should be carrying a tiny cucumber with a flower at the tip. Nip out the end of the shoot, one or two leaves beyond the developing fruit. Check plants twice a week – nip out the tips of sideshoots and tie up the main stems to keep them under control. They grow very fast. If you don't mind having lots of smallish cucumbers, then nipping out sideshoots and thinning fruit is less important.

Keep them happy by...

Giving them a warm, sunny, sheltered spot, especially outdoors. The plants are not hardy and hate cold, wet, windy conditions. Be very careful not to over-water young plants, but do make sure you provide plenty of water when they are cropping. It's essential to keep plants growing steadily otherwise developing cucumbers may abort.

Worth trying...

'Burpless' – An unromantic name, but a good description; tender, crunchy, medium-sized fruit. This F1 hybrid is the best of all the outdoor varieties.
'Carmen' – Heavy-cropping, F1 hybrid for the greenhouse; resistant to powdery mildew and several other diseases.
'Crystal Lemon' – Heavy-cropping outdoor variety with small, round, yellow fruits. One plant is enough.
'Flamingo' – An all-female F1 hybrid for the greenhouse; slender, long fruits.

'Long White' – Mild-flavoured outdoor variety with short, cream-skinned fruits.

'Passandra' – All-female F1 mini cucumber – the fruits reach 15cm (6in) long; disease-resistant; grow under cover.

Enjoy them...

The cucumbers are ready as soon as their shape fills out all the way along and they look big enough. You can eat them while quite tiny and they're delicious, but it takes practise to know exactly when the flesh turns from being slightly tangy to being juicy – it's when they're about the circumference of a 10p piece. Use secateurs to snip through the narrow stem connecting the cucumber to the plant – don't pull or twist them off or you'll drag the plant down or break off long lengths of stem that should carry the next lot of cucumbers.

Look out for...

The plants are susceptible to powdery mildew which may appear at the end of the season (*see* courgettes, pages 84–5). Choose disease-resistant varieties.

Cucumber mosaic virus can sometimes infect plants (*see* courgettes, pages 84–5), so choose virus-resistant varieties where possible.

Red spider mites invade crops under glass. They spin minute webs and suck the sap from the leaves, which begin to yellow. Discourage them by keeping the atmosphere damp; if necessary, use a biological control (*see* page 53).

Sex discrimination

It is easier to grow all-female hybrid varieties of cucumber. With other varieties the risk of pollination is great and this makes the fruit bitter and full of seeds. If you must try them, put insect-proof screens over all greenhouse openings to keep out pollinating insects. Remove male flowers every few days – they're the ones without a baby cucumber growing behind them.

'Burpless' is a long-standing, well-proven outdoor variety. If you want classic straight green fruit, it will do you proud. This particular plant is being grown up a decorative wicker obelisk – an alternative to runner beans for bringing height to a potager.

Endive

SOW MAY, JUN, JUL
harvest JAN, FEB, MAR AND SEP, OCT, NOV, DEC

Endive is like chicory in flavour and use but it is very different in appearance, with frizzy leaves in loose heads. If you like the bitter taste, it is a useful salad crop as it grows through the winter, making you less likely to have to trot down to the supermarket for a bag of sterilized green leaves.

Cultivation

DIFFICULTY Intermediate; get the details right and it's fine.
SOW In situ in rows 30cm (12in) apart from mid-spring; make successive sowings to have endive from early autumn to spring.
SPACE 30cm (12in) apart by gradual thinning.
CARE Water sparingly, increasing the supply slightly as plants mature. Plants remaining in the ground as winter approaches won't need watering, as rainfall should be adequate.
YIELD A 1.5m (5ft) row will produce 5–6 heads.
STORAGE Leave in the ground until they are needed.

Keep them happy by…

Protecting plants that you intend to harvest through the winter. They will usually do quite well until late winter, but you can help by covering them with cloches or fleece for protection until you are ready to blanch them (*see* box, below).

Worth trying…

'Moss Curled' – Called 'frisée' in France; large heads of filigree foliage; tender and tasty when blanched. 'Kentucky' is similar.

Enjoy them…

By cutting the whole plant at the stem just above the ground. Trim off the tough outer leaves. Use the soft, tender, yellowish leaves at the centre of the rosette.

Look out for…

Slugs and snails like to hide inside blanching pots, where they snack on the tender heads of endive; check the blanching pots regularly and remove slugs by hand, but also take anti-slug and snail precautions throughout the growing season (*see* pages 52–5).

Blanching

When they are three months old, choose a few of the biggest plants to blanch. Blanching helps to reduce bitterness in the flavour of the leaves. Stand a heavy bucket or large clay flowerpot (with drainage hole blocked up) upside down over the top. Leave the pot in place for three weeks.

Alternatively, bunch up the outer leaves round the heart and use raffia or soft string to tie them in place – the result will be slightly less pale, but you will have fewer problems with worms or slugs. When one batch is ready, start to blanch a few more.

A few crunchy endive leaves drizzled with salad dressing and popped between two slices of granary bread make a good snack lunch.

Home-grown endives may not reach the prodigious size of those you can buy in a French market, but 'Moss Curled' will provide enough leaves to keep you happy.

Florence fennel

Under cover
sow APR **plant** JUN, JULY
harvest AUG, SEP

Outdoors
sow MAY **plant** JUN, JUL
harvest AUG, SEP

The swollen white bases of Florence fennel plants taste like aniseed and provide a touch of class when used raw in salads; they are even better cooked, particularly roasted with other vegetables in olive oil. It is not always reliable, especially in dodgy summers, and is easiest to raise under cover.

Cultivation

DIFFICULTY Advanced; not time consuming but demanding.
SOW Start plants off indoors in spring; sow three seeds each in small pots. Remove two and keep the strongest seedling.
PLANT Harden off seedlings carefully before planting in a greenhouse border or polytunnel in late spring, or outside in a sunny, sheltered spot from midsummer – wait for a prolonged warm spell.
SPACE 23–30cm (9–12in) apart in each direction.
CARE Water carefully – they need little water at first but must not dry out. As they grow and the weather warms up, increase watering and ensure the soil stays moist at all times. Feed with a general-purpose feed. Cover outdoor-grown plants with fleece at night if it's chilly, even in summer.

Keep them happy by…

It's essential to grow plants fast and without a check or the 'bulbs' will be too tough and the plants will bolt prematurely.

Worth trying…

'Goal' – F1 hybrid, produces large bulbs with a good aromatic fennel flavour.
'Victorio' – Fast-growing F1 hybrid variety with short, squat bases.

Enjoy them…

When they are the size of a tennis ball. Don't delay, or by the time you've used one or two the rest will have bolted. Pull the whole plant up, trim off the root and lower leaves and cut the foliage back to a few centimetres above the top of the 'bulb'.

Look out for…

Bolting is their main pastime, making them useless for eating. Any little discomfort sets them off – dry soil, poor growing conditions, lack of organic matter, sudden swings in temperature…all have an effect.

Slugs and some underground pests also enjoy them (*see* pages 52–5 for controls).

If you can grow Florence fennel well, you will have every reason to be proud of yourself. They are a challenge, but worth it if you like the flavour.

Garlic

plant FEB, MAR AND NOV
harvest JUN, JUL, AUG

This little health-giving, breath-affecting bulb needs no introduction. It is an excellent addition to the vegetable garden and good value for time. If you grow onions, you can grow garlic. Don't plant garlic bought from the greengrocer's: choose properly prepared bulbs from a garden centre or seed catalogue.

Cultivation

DIFFICULTY Easy; low input.
PLANT whole cloves, ideally in late autumn. Autumn-planted garlic is ready earlier and usually makes larger bulbs, since it has a longer growing season. Choose the biggest cloves for planting and discard tiny ones. Push the cloves into the soil so the tip is a couple of centimetres (1in) below the surface.
SPACE 15cm (6in) apart in each direction.
CARE Check occasionally and carefully replant any cloves the birds pull up. Water both autumn- and spring-planted garlic in dry spells in summer.
YIELD A 1.5m (5ft) row produces about 10 bulbs.
STORAGE Some varieties store well, others need using quite quickly. (*See* Worth trying, right.) 'Wet' garlic is like a fresh vegetable and needs using promptly.

Keep them happy by…

Drying them well after harvesting and storing them in the house rather than a shed, where the cooler atmosphere may start them into growth.

Worth trying…

'Lautrec Wight' – Pink cloves with a white skin; stores until early spring.
'Purple Wight' – Early variety with purple-tinged cloves, ready for use 'wet' from early summer. Stores until early winter.
'Solent Wight' – Bred for the British climate; ready from midsummer.
'Purple Modovan' – Vintage, very pungent variety with mauve-tinged skin; use within four months.

Enjoy them…

From early summer as 'wet' garlic – the plants are still leafy but there are reasonable-sized heads underground. Pull only what you need. Harvest the rest when the foliage starts to dry off naturally – midsummer (autumn-planted) or late summer (spring-planted). When it has turned brown, dig up the plants and let them finish drying off on the ground in the sun. Try slicing up the stalks and using them as you would the cloves.

Look out for…

Rust disease (red spots on the foliage) can kill the leaves prematurely, resulting in smaller heads of garlic. It's often worse on ground that is poorly drained or rich in nitrogen fertilizer, but particularly where members of the onion family have been grown before, or debris from infected plants has been left behind or is in the compost. Destroy affected foliage, don't grow the onion family in that site for 4–5 years, and practise strict crop rotation (*see* page 23).

Bolting sometimes just happens. Don't worry about it: some varieties bolt easily but it doesn't affect their ability to produce a good bulb.

Garlic has been grown commercially on the Isle of Wight for many years, which accounts for the names, although the varieties probably originated elsewhere. 'Solent Wight' is a pale-cloved bulb ready to use from midsummer.

Elephant garlic

Elephant garlic is not a true garlic, being more closely related to leeks. It has a thick stem and a huge underground 'head', up to 10cm (4in) across, of a few enormous cloves. It is brilliant for roasting and has a sweet mild flavour. Use within four months.

Kale

SOW APR, MAY, JUN **plant** MAY, JUN, JUL
harvest JAN, FEB, MAR, APR AND DEC

Kale is a member of the cabbage (brassica) family, but
has its own characteristic flavour and softer leaves that
wilt to be delicate and tender when steamed. If you are
looking to eat vegetables in season, then it is a must as it
is harvested through the winter months, when few other
fresh veg are available.

Cultivation

DIFFICULTY Easy; low input.

SOW in pots or seed trays.

PLANT Transplant into beds as and when the seedlings are
large enough to handle.

SPACE 45cm (18in) apart in each direction.

CARE Keep watered in dry spells through the summer.

YIELD Up to 1kg (2¼lb) per plant.

STORAGE Keep leaves on the plant until needed.

Keep them happy by...

Planting in firm soil – after all, kale is a brassica and this is what
brassicas like.

Worth trying...

'Black Tuscany' ('Nero di Toscana') – Upright plants (can be
spaced 30cm/12in apart); rich flavour from long and narrow,
bobbly deep-green leaves. It can be picked from late summer
to early spring of the following year.

'Pentland Brig' – Tender, tasty, dual-purpose curly kale: pick
leaves in winter and the succulent shoots in spring; use the
latter like broccoli spears.

'Redbor' – Bronze-purple curly kale with crinkly leaves that can
be used young in salads.

Enjoy them...

By picking a few leaves as soon as they are big enough, but
don't take too many at once. Take your main harvest from early
winter (from a mid-spring sowing) onwards. Leave the plants in
situ over winter, as they enjoy a new spurt of growth in spring
and produce a quick crop of succulent young leaves before
running to seed.

Look out for...

Caterpillars can be a nuisance, but they are less of a problem
with kale than on many other brassica crops. Remove them by
hand or use an organic pesticide; keep the plants covered with
insect-proof mesh if it's a real problem.

Clubroot is an ever-present threat (*see* page 74).

Though lacking the exotic appearance of some of its relatives,
'Pentland Brig' is a reliable kale with plenty of flavour.

Kohl rabi

SOW APR, MAY, JUN
harvest JUL, AUG, SEP

This odd-ball vegetable tastes like a mild turnip when cooked, slightly sweeter raw. If you like it, you should give it a go as you'll rarely find it in the shops; if you don't know it, grow it for something unusual to show your friends – you'll probably end up liking it too.

Cultivation

DIFFICULTY Intermediate; medium input.
SOW in situ from mid-spring.
SPACE Gradually thin out plants to 15cm (6in) apart in each direction.
CARE Keep well watered throughout the life of the crop – it's vital the plants never have a check to their growth, otherwise you'll end up with tough hard balls of fibrous matter.
YIELD A 1.5m (5ft) row produces about 10 'balls'.
STORAGE Keeps for up to two weeks in the fridge.

Keep them happy by...

Providing well-prepared, fertile soil with plenty of rich organic matter.

Worth trying...

'Blue Delicacy' – late purple variety of kohl rabi with a mild, turnip-like flavour.
'Kolibri' – Purple globes with white flesh; a juicy F1 hybrid.
'Logo' – Fast growing with white globes; slow to bolt.
'Supershmelze' – Green globes with white flesh; can grow huge, but is not widely available.

Enjoy them...

When the first globes reach golf-ball size (use these raw); work through the crop, eating them all before they reach tennis-ball size. Pull up whole plants, top-and-tail the globes and peel as thinly as you can.

> You can grow purple, white or green kohl rabi – they all taste similar, it's just the colour that alters. The different colours do best at different temperatures; white kohl rabi for early crops and purple for later in the season.

Look out for...

It can develop a woody texture, splitting or bolting due to poor growing conditions or a shortage of water.

Clubroot (*see* page 74) could attack, but as the plant grows quickly it is rare. Luckily, caterpillars are not that partial to the leaves either.

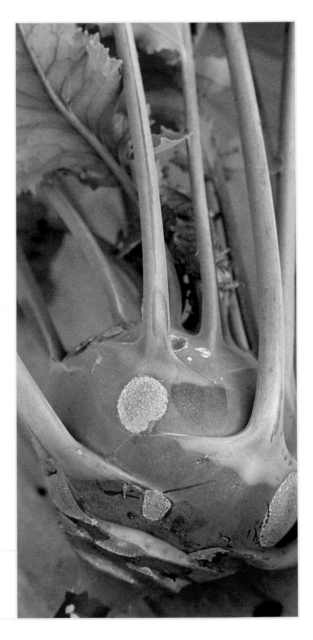

Leeks

SOW MAR, APR **plant** JUN
harvest JAN, FEB, MAR AND SEP, OCT, NOV, DEC

Leeks are one of those vegetables that are perennially in vogue, and it's easy to see why. Tasty with a good texture, they are extremely versatile in cooking, have a long cropping season and are easy to grow. Grow two or three different varieties to have continuous supplies right through autumn, winter and early spring, and grow summer baby leeks too.

Cultivation

DIFFICULTY Easy; little input.

SOW in seed beds in spring.

PLANT Transplant seedlings when they reach 15–20cm (6–8in) tall.

SPACE 15cm (6in) apart, in rows 30cm (12in) apart.

CARE Plant into fairly firm soil: make a hole 7.5–10cm (3–4in) deep for each seedling using a big dibber or a thick piece of cane. Drop each seedling in place without firming the soil around the roots. 'Puddle' them in with a watering can so the planting holes fill with water.

YIELD A 1.5m (5ft) row produces about 2kg (4½lb).

STORAGE Leave in the ground until needed; they keep in the fridge for up to a week.

Keep them happy by...

Providing good growing conditions and plenty of water. Bolting can occur if plants aren't completely happy.

Worth trying...

'Apollo' – An F1 hybrid with good rust resistance; bred for winter use.

'King Richard' – An early cropper (early autumn to early winter); long, slender stems.

'Musselburgh' – A reliable old variety that withstands hard winters; early winter to early spring.

'Porbella' – Good cropper over a long season from mid-autumn to late winter.

Enjoy them...

A few at a time as soon as they reach a usable size. If you are growing several varieties, it makes sense to use the earlier maturing ones first as they won't last so well through winter.

Look out for...

Just like onions and garlic, leeks are prone to bolting. Some years are worse than others. Use bolters instantly, even if they are still small, otherwise they'll be inedible. Leeks sown very early indoors (in midwinter), tend to produce more bolters than those sown outside in late spring.

They suffer rust, as do all members of the onion family (*see* garlic, page 90); salvage what you can by harvesting leeks to use early. Look out for rust-resistant varieties.

Baby leeks

'King Richard' gives a naturally early crop of long, slender leeks and is ideal for raising babies. Prepare the ground well – as for a seed bed (*see* page 36). Sow thinly, making several sowings at three-weekly intervals from early spring to early summer. Thin the seedlings to 2.5cm (1in) apart, but don't transplant. Water carefully and give a regular feed with a general-purpose liquid feed. Start pulling baby leeks when they resemble spring onions. They'll crop from early summer until early autumn. If you have a polytunnel, a sowing in early spring will give you a late spring crop.

Right the way through the winter, leeks can be harvested. Only when the ground is frozen will they be unavailable.

Lettuce and various salad leaves

Aside from the lettuces, there is a wide variety of other leafy plants that can be grown for use in salads (some are also suitable for stir fries and braising). You can grow the plants individually or as a mixed sowing for 'cut-and-come-again'; pre-mixed seed packets are available. Most are easy to grow and can have a long cropping period from successional sowings, (*see* page 43) it's a matter of you choosing the varieties you like best and having a go.

Lettuces and salad leaves make an attractive display in the garden – but they're also irresistable to slugs and snails, so you do need to be vigilant.

Cultivation

DIFFICULTY Most are easy to grow well, some need a little attention.
SOW Make early sowings in pots or seed trays in a propagator, on a windowsill, or in a cold greenhouse. Prick seedlings out into pots and transplant as the weather improves.
SPACE According to the variety, but usually in rows 30cm (12in) apart.
CARE Lettuces and lettuce-based mixtures need plenty of water and good soil, the rest mostly like water but are less fussy about soil conditions.

Look out for…

Slugs and snails are a big threat to most salad leaves. Take precautions continuously, using a biological control from several weeks before sowing (*see* page 53).

Flea beetles make pinprick holes in many salad leaves, especially if the spring and early summer are dry. Attacks rarely kill plants, but the damaged foliage looks uninviting in a salad bowl. Help plants to get established by good soil preparation and generous watering; cover with insect-proof mesh (*see* page 52). Greenfly may take a shine to lettuce and lamb's lettuce in particular; brush them off to prevent a build up (*see* page 53).

With pre-mixed salad leaf seeds, one variety is often stronger or faster growing than anything else. When you spot the culprit, hoick some of it out while it is young to maintain a better balance of leaf types.

Bolting can occur in hot or dry conditions, particularly in poor soil; remove bolted plants to the compost heap as the salad leaves will taste bitter.

Chinese mustard greens

SOW MAY, JUN, JUL, AUG
harvest JUN, JUL, AUG, SEP, OCT

These are members of the cabbage family and like firm soil and similar growing conditions to other brassicas. They can be grown under cover or protected by gardener's fleece for a longer season. They are suitable for cooking or eating raw in salads.

SPACE 15–20cm (6–8in) apart.
HARVEST As you thin out young leaves, take alternate plants to eat as babies, leaving the rest to grow larger.

The hot, spicy leaves of fresh Chinese mustard greens.

Lamb's lettuce Corn salad, mâche

SOW JAN, FEB, MAR AND SEP, OCT, NOV, DEC
harvest JAN, FEB, MAR, APR AND OCT, NOV, DEC

Providing salad
leaves through the
winter, lamb's lettuce
is best grown under
cover or protected
with fleece.

SPACE 2.5cm (1in)
apart, in rows 15cm
(6in) apart.
HARVEST when plants
are 2.5cm (1in) across.

Tasty lamb's lettuce.

Mizuna

SOW MAY, JUN, JUL, AUG
harvest JUN, JUL, AUG, SEP, OCT

This is a member of
the cabbage family
and likes similar
growing conditions
to other brassicas.

SPACE 30cm (12in)
apart.
HARVEST Use the
plants as cut-and-come-
again and they will
provide leaves through
the winter.

Young mizuna leaves.

Lettuce

SOW MAR, APR, MAY **plant** APR, MAY
harvest JUN, JUL, AUG, SEP, OCT

The best-known salad vegetable comes in a wide choice
of forms, colours, and leaf shapes. Prefers rich, fertile,
loose soil. Keep
weeds down and
water well.

SPACE According to
variety.
HARVEST Hearting
types are best enjoyed
when they have formed
a heart; others can be
eaten as soon as they're
big enough.

Neat conical heads of
'Cos' lettuce.

Pak choi

SOW APR, MAY, JUN, JUL, AUG
harvest JUN, JUL, AUG, SEP, OCT

A member of the cabbage family and requiring similar
conditions to other brassicas, pak choi is a great salad
vegetable but also wonderful braised or steamed.

SPACE 15–20cm
(6–8in) apart.
HARVEST Start pulling
whole plants as soon as
the bases swell to 2.5cm
(1in) in diameter,
otherwise the last leaves
will have become coarse
by the time you get to
eat them.

Crunchy pak choi.

Purslane

SOW MAR, APR, MAY, JUN, JUL
harvest APR, MAY, JUN, JUL, AUG, SEP, OCT, NOV

Unlike other salad leaves, purslane has succulent foliage and can cope with hot, dry summers. The seeds may be more difficult than other salads to obtain.

SPACE 7.5cm (3in) apart, in rows 23cm (9in) apart.
HARVEST A few leaves at a time; the plants will continue growing and providing leaves throughout summer.

Succulent purslane leaves.

Rocket

SOW MAR, APR, MAY, JUN, JUL, AUG, SEP
harvest APR, MAY, JUN, JUL, AUG, SEP, OCT, NOV

Another member of the cabbage family, but this one grows under almost any conditions, even on a bright windowsill through winter.

SPACE 10–15cm (4–6in) apart.
HARVEST Pick a few leaves from each plant and leave them to grow; watch out for bolting.

Well-grown rocket.

Onions

Spring onions
SOW MAR, APR, MAY, JUN, JUL
harvest JUN, JUL, AUG, SEP

Winter-hardy spring onions
SOW AUG, SEP, OCT
harvest FEB, MAR, APR, MAY, JUN

Bulb onions – summer, from sets
plant MAR, APR
harvest AUG, SEP

Bulb onions – overwintering, from sets
plant SEP, OCT
harvest MAY, JUN, JUL

Onions are a nice easy crop to grow and you can have something oniony to harvest pretty much all year if you're clever. They might be reasonably cheap in the shops but it's not like eating your own. And it is great to have spring onions and red onions on the doorstep; both make an ordinary salad into something special, as well as being great for cooking.

Cultivation

DIFFICULTY Easy; little input.
SOW a short row of spring onions every 3–4 weeks from early spring to midsummer, then sow an overwintering variety from late summer to mid-autumn. Sow thinly and thin out if the seedlings are overcrowded.
PLANT maincrop (summer) onion sets in early spring, and overwintering onion sets in autumn.
SPACE Thin spring onions to 2.5cm (1in) apart, and allow 15cm (6in) between rows. Plant onion sets 10cm (4in) apart, in rows 20cm (8in) apart.
CARE Keep plants watered in dry spells so they don't suffer a check to their growth, which may encourage bolting.
YIELD Depends on the variety; about 1.3–1.8kg (3–4lb) from a 1.5m (5ft) row.
STORAGE Most maincrops will remain in good condition from early autumn until late winter. Keep them in the light to avoid sprouting. Use overwintering onions within a month or so after they have been harvested.

It's worth growing 'Red Baron' for its appearance alone, but it is also a good cropper and keeps well.

Keep them happy by...

Weeding regularly; when you plant, make sure your onion hoe will fit between your rows, to make weeding less of a chore. Keep the soil evenly moist when they are growing.

Worth trying...

'Garnet' – Maincrop, new version of 'Red Baron'; slightly earlier to mature.

'North Holland Blood Red' ('Redmate') – Reliable, purplish red spring onion for spring sowing; grows on to produce red onions that keep until the following spring.

'Overwintering White Lisbon' – Very hardy spring onion, reliable for autumn sowing in the open (protect with fleece ideally) but best under (cool) cover.

'Radar' – Gold-skinned overwintering onion; good for cold areas or bad weather.

'Red Baron' – Maincrop (summer) red onion with a fantastic flavour, mild enough for salads; keeps well through winter.

'Rosanna' – An improved version of an old favourite maincrop; pink flesh and red-brown skin.

'Senshyu' – Japanese overwintering onion with semi-flattened bulbs.

'Sturon' – Reliable, tasty maincrop (summer) onion; bolt resistant; keeps well through winter.

'White Lisbon' – Classic, white-skinned spring onion for spring/ summer sowing; grows on to produce white, silver-skin-type golf-ball-sized onions.

Enjoy them...

As soon as they are big enough. Use the thinnings of spring onions as you would chives, then pull alternate plants as baby spring onions; any left to grow can be used like mild onions. With maincrops, bend the tops over once the leaves start naturally turning yellow or brown to assist ripening; lift the bulbs when completely ripe and leave them in the sun to finish drying before storing in shallow trays in an airy shed. Use overwintering onions fresh from the ground from the time the first few reach usable size (around late spring); keep pulling them as needed.

Look out for...

As with all members of the family, bolting is a problem in some seasons. Choose a bolt-resistant variety and, where possible, buy heat-treated sets, which reduces the risk of bolting.

Mildew, a white or grey fungal growth, is disfiguring and debilitating. Cut off affected foliage and do not store bulbs.

White rot, an unpleasant disease, is quite common in onions, including spring onions; it spreads rapidly and has no cure. The foliage of affected plants turns yellow, then white cotton-wool-like stuff with black blobs in it develops near the base of the plant. The fungus that causes white rot remains in the soil so you won't be able to grow members of the onion family there for years (some say 8, others about 20). Destroy affected plants and foliage and grow onions elsewhere. Practise crop rotation (see page 23) to minimize the risk of the disease occurring.

Seed or sets?

As onion seed is short-lived and must be sown fresh, it seems sensible to let someone else take on the task of sowing it. Commercial growers raise young onions until they have made small bulbs called sets. At this point, like any other bulb, they can be harvested and sold. Sets are simply small onions which, when planted, become quickly established and grow into proper-sized onions without the hassle of growing onions from seed.

Parsnips

SOW MAR
harvest OCT, NOV, DEC

Baby-size parsnips
SOW MAR
harvest JUL, AUG, SEP

When you grow traditional parsnips, you have to be patient as they take about nine months to reach hearty roasting size, and they need space. But you can enjoy parsnips much sooner as babies, which take up much less space and save you a packet on what you would pay in the shops. You will need proper baby-parsnip seed as normal parsnip seedlings stay very thin until quite late in their life, so cannot be eaten early.

'Avonresister' is one of the best varieties to grow if you're worried about canker and prefer small portions.

Cultivation

DIFFICULTY Intermediate; low input.

SOW Thinly, about 2.5cm (1in) apart, in situ in deep, rich, fertile soil where manure was not used the previous winter; wait for mild weather if the soil is cold and wet.

SPACE Thin 'normal' parsnips to 15cm (6in) in several stages, babies to 5cm (2in). Space the rows 30cm (12in) apart, less to produce baby veg.

CARE Water in dry spells and weed regularly.

YIELD A 1.5m (5ft) row produces about 1.8kg (4lb); less for babies.

STORAGE Leave them in the ground until needed unless it's very wet, in which case lift them and store in a frost-free shed.

Keep them happy by...

Giving them a well-prepared site that has been deeply dug, is not too stony and has not recently (within the last year) been manured. On stony soil, build a raised bed (see pages 18–20). Fanged roots (they are still edible) will be more common if you can't provide these growing conditions.

Worth trying...

'Arrow' and 'Dagger' – Good baby varieties; but try other new baby varieties too.

'Avonresister' – One of the stalwarts of the veg garden; resistant to canker, less likely than most to bolt in adverse conditions and produces good crops even on poor ground. Smallish roots, so space 7.5–10cm (3–4in) apart.

'Tender and True' – The one for flavour; long roots with small cores.

Enjoy them...

From summer (babies) onwards. Dig up roots as required (after the foliage starts turning yellow).

Look out for...

Parsnips can be affected by canker. The roots develop brown scabs, especially round the top, which eat into the flesh. Less-damaged roots can be used once the canker is removed, but some are ruined. It is thought that canker may be caused by too much organic matter or by too much or too little rain. There is no cure; grow canker-resistant varieties, such as 'Avonresister'.

Plants may bolt, making the root fibrous and inedible. It's down to poor growing conditions, sometimes the gardener's fault, sometimes not.

Peas

Early varieties
SOW MAR, APR AND JUN, JUL
harvest JUN, JUL AND SEP, OCT

Maincrop varieties
SOW APR, MAY, JUN, JUL
harvest JUL, AUG, SEP

Mangetout and sugarsnaps
SOW APR, MAY, JUN
harvest JUN, JUL, AUG, SEP

If you want to grow peas, from a time, effort, and result point of view it is best to stick to mangetout and sugar snap types, which are much better than the shop offerings – to say nothing of being less travelled. Shelling podded peas is fun, but it is difficult to do maincrop peas as well as the 'two hours from picked to frozen' brigade, who have the help of all sorts of high-tech equipment. Mangetout and sugar snaps are unaffected by maggots, which can ruin whole crops of 'normal' peas.

Cultivation

DIFFICULTY Intermediate; reasonable input.
SOW Make two or three staggered rows in a flat-bottomed drill about 20cm (8in) wide, so the seeds are about 7.5cm (3in) apart in each direction.
PLANT If you have raised early crops under cover, plant them out in staggered rows, with plants 10–15cm (4–6in) apart in each direction.
SPACE 45cm (18in) between sets of rows for short varieties; 90cm (3ft) for tall varieties, to allow access.
CARE Keep plants watered in dry weather and weed regularly.
YIELD A 1.5m (5ft) row produces about 2.3kg (5lb).
STORAGE Eat fresh. If you want to keep them, freeze them as soon as you pick them (*see* Storage, pages 58–9).

Keep them happy by...

Providing plant support. After sowing, push pea sticks in along the rows of short-growing varieties. Tall varieties are best with 2m (6ft) posts and horizontal wires holding up pea netting.

Worth trying...

'Alderman' – Traditional, 2m (6ft) tall, shelling variety, late to start cropping, but productive over a much longer cropping season than dwarf pea plants. Sow early spring to midsummer.
'Feltham First' – Round-seeded shelling pea suitable for the very earliest sowings in late winter. These dwarf plants, 45cm (18in) tall, need little support.
'Golden Sweet' – Tall mangetout (2m/6ft) with mauve flowers, pale green leaves, red leaf nodes and yellow pods; very decorative, so great for a potager (*see* page 15).
'Hurst Green Shaft' – A delicious second-early or maincrop variety, 75cm (2½ft) tall. Long and heavy cropping.
'Kelvedon Wonder' – Wrinkle-seeded shelling variety on dwarf plants 45cm (18in) tall with good flavour. Sow early spring to midsummer; ideal if you only want to buy one packet of pea seed.
'Oregon Sugar Pod' – Tall mangetout reaching 1m (40in) tall, with a fairly long cropping season; grow outdoors from early spring to midsummer, or early/late under cover.
'Sugar Ann' – Tall sugar snap variety, 1.5m (5ft) high; needs support but crops for a reasonable length of time.

Who could resist a pea like this? 'Hurst Green Shaft' living up to its descriptive name with its young peas just beginning to swell.

'Sugar Snap' – Early sugar snap variety; dwarf 75cm (2½ft) tall so needs little support; can be sown early under cover.

Enjoy them…

When they reach a usable size. Mangetout pods are best at 5cm (2in) long; they never get fat but they can get stringy, so pick and discard any that have 'gone beyond it'. Sugar snaps are best at about 4cm (1½in) long but can be shelled if they've grown too large. Check the progress of shelling peas by popping open one or two of the biggest pods – use them while young, tender, and sweet; don't let them grow big, they get tough and starchy.

Look out for…

Seeds may be eaten by mice or other rodents, and can succumb to cold, wet soil at sowing time.

Powdery mildew (grey-white talc-like powder) on young leaves and tips of shoots can spread to cover whole plants. Old plants and any under cover are prone, and it is worst on dry soil. Keep plants well watered and ensure good air circulation.

Pea weevil makes irregular notches in the margins of leaves; all but the most badly infested young seedlings nearly always

Continuous cropping – for pea fans

■ Plant early and late-shelling pea varieties and make successional sowings for a long season, or choose a tall heritage variety, such as 'Alderman', which has a longer season.
■ Plant tall mangetout varieties; these should crop for six weeks or more.

grow out of it without problems. The weevils, if you spot them, are 6mm (¼in) long and buff-brown with six legs and a short pair of forward-facing antennae.

Maggot larvae of the pea moth tunnel into the pods of shelling peas to eat the seeds and deposit their mess. They can ruin a whole crop of plants at the same time. Either sow early or late, as these crops seem to be less susceptible, or use insect mesh (see page 52). Mangetout and sugar snap peas don't seem to be affected.

Foot-and-root rot kills the roots – they turn black and the young plants turn yellow. It may be due to overwatering poorly established small plants in cold, dull weather, or an organism in the soil. Put new seeds or plants in a different patch of ground and practise crop rotation (see page 23).

For peas out of season

Sow all varieties in trays of multipurpose compost in a cold greenhouse or cool windowsill indoors in late winter.

Shelling peas Harden off seedlings before planting out in a mild spell about a month later. Protect young plants with gardener's fleece (see page 39). Round-seeded varieties (it'll say on the packet) are best for very early sowings (gamblers might even like to sow them in autumn to overwinter outdoors and produce an early spring crop – results are not guaranteed).

Sugar snaps and mangetout Plant in a greenhouse or polytunnel border once the weather turns milder, usually from late winter. In early spring, sow a few rows of pea seed in situ under cover.

It's also worth sowing a wide row of 'Oregon Sugar Pod' mangetout into a polytunnel border in autumn; plants should overwinter, even if they look rather ropey, to produce a very early crop the following spring.

The secret of growing mangetout and sugar snap peas is to harvest them young and crisp before the pods become tough or stringy.

Peppers

SOW FEB, MAR plant MAY, JUN
harvest JUN, JUL, AUG, SEPT

Home-grown peppers are like a more concentrated version of the ones you can buy in the supermarket; they are perhaps less thick-fleshed and juicy, but far more flavoursome. It is easy to get the green fruit, but ripening to red is more likely on indoor plants than those peppers grown outdoors.

Cultivation

DIFFICULTY Easy; little input.

SOW in a heated propagator or on a windowsill indoors at 21–27°C (70–80°F). Prick out the seedlings into individual small pots when large enough to handle, and grow on at 16–19°C (60–65°F).

PLANT Transfer the young plants to an unheated greenhouse in late spring or put them outdoors in early to midsummer. Harden off before planting out – they are frost-tender.

SPACE 45cm (18in) apart; they can grow individually in pots or two to a growbag.

CARE Water in after planting, then water sparingly until plants are growing strongly and starting to flower or bear fruit.

Keep them happy by…

Feeding weekly with liquid tomato feed after the first flower opens to encourage plenty of fruit. Support plants by tying the main stem to a cane (*see* page 56).

Worth trying…

'Bell Boy' – Heavy cropping and reliable, often sold as plants in garden centres. The fruits start green, ripening to red. There are other 'Bells' in various colours.

'Big Banana' – Long, tapering peppers to 25cm (10in). Green, ripening through yellow to red.

'Matador' – Bull-horn-shaped sweet peppers; red when ripe.

'Redskin' – Compact, bushy plants, good for containers, with large numbers of oblong green peppers, ripening to red.

Enjoy them…

Green as soon as they are big enough to use – they probably won't grow as big as the ones you buy in the shops. If you want red peppers, leave green peppers to ripen, but be aware the plant won't produce any more fruit during this time. For a larger crop, it is best to use them green and then red. To pick, don't tug or twist since the branches are easily damaged.

Look out for…

Greenfly affect peppers, especially youngsters under cover. Check plants regularly and wipe off greenfly with damp tissue, or use an organic insect spray.

Outdoor plants can fail to produce fruit if growing conditions are poor (lack of sun, cold, dull or windy weather); overwatering can also cause crop failure. In a poor summer, try to move them into a conservatory or enclosed porch for shelter, or drape them with fleece at night and on cold or windy days, for extra protection.

A green pepper ready for harvesting. Cut the short stem with secateurs to avoid damaging the plant.

Potatoes

First earlies
chit FEB, MAR plant MAR, APR
harvest MAY, JUN, JUL

Second earlies
chit FEB, MAR plant APR
harvest JUN, JUL, AUG SEP

Maincrop
plant APR
harvest SEP, OCT, NOV

Today, a huge range of potato varieties is available to gardeners: bakers, chippers, mashers, salad spuds, novelty and coloured ones, and heirloom varieties – as well as a selection of disease-resistant ones, ideal for organic growing.

Spuds are not grown from seed, nor from any sprouted leftovers you have in your vegetable rack. Instead, you must buy 'seed' potatoes, which are available from garden centres and via mail order in late winter or early spring. These are tubers grown especially for the job and certified disease-free. The ideal seed potato is the size of a hen's egg, but you will find bigger and smaller ones.

Potatoes are known as first earlies (new potatoes), second earlies and maincrop, depending on how early or late in the season they are ready for harvesting. It is traditional to 'chit' first and second early varieties (*see* box) to get them started into growth before planting them out when the weather warms up a little. This gives them a head start as their growing season is shortish. You don't need to chit maincrop spuds, since they have a much longer growing season.

Cultivation

DIFFICULTY Easy; little input apart from regular earthing up (*see* how to earth up, page 63).
PLANT First earlies in early spring; second-earlies a week later and maincrop potatoes a week after that. Plant all tubers 13cm (5in) deep.
SPACE Earlies 30cm (12in) apart in rows 60cm (24in) apart; second-earlies and maincrops 40cm (15in) apart in rows 75cm (2½ft) apart.
CARE Hoe between rows to keep down weeds until the potato shoots are 15cm (6in) high, then earth up the plants (*see* how to earth up, page 63). If frost threatens, earth up as soon as the

Chitting

Chitting involves sitting the tubers in a box, such as an old egg box or seed tray, with the growing end facing upwards – recognizable by the cluster of tiny buds ('eyes') on it. Keep them in good light but out of direct sunlight. When the shoots are 1–2.5cm (½–1in) long, the potatoes are ready for planting.

shoots appear above ground. Except in a long dry summer, you shouldn't need to water potatoes.
YIELD Much depends on variety.
STORAGE Harvest first and second earlies as you need them; they are fine in a cool place for a week or so. Store maincrops, dry and with the soil brushed off, in brown paper or hessian sacks in a cool dark place.

Keep them happy by...

Checking for signs of slug damage. Potatoes are popular with keeled slugs. These live underground and burrow into the tubers, making them prone to rotting. Slugs love organic matter, particularly if it isn't very well rotted, so only plant potatoes on ground that had compost or manure dug in at the start of the previous season. Use the biological control for slugs (*see* page 53); using slug pellets on the soil surface has little or no effect on keeled slugs. Where slug damage is a regular problem, look for potato varieties with in-bred slug resistance.

Worth trying...
FIRST EARLIES

'Duke of York' – Pale yellow tubers for new potatoes or to grow on as later maincrop potatoes; a good choice if you only have room for one variety.

'Foremost' – Firm, waxy, white, salad new potato. Eat hot or cold.
'Mimi' – Small, pink-flushed tubers; compact foliage makes this ideal for container growing.
'Pentland Javelin' – Delicious white waxy potato, ideal salad potato; disease resistant.
'Rocket' – Fast-growing early; large crops of round white tubers; disease resistant. Try it very early under cover.

SECOND EARLIES

'Charlotte' – An attractive and highly popular, superb salad potato with golden skin and firm, waxy, cream-coloured flesh.
'Edzell Blue' – Purplish skin gives this tasty Victorian variety its name. The very floury white flesh makes it a fabulous masher; it tends to crumble when boiled.
'Estima' – Large oval, yellow-fleshed tubers, excellent as summer bakers; plants do well even in dry summers.
'International Kidney' – Of 'Jersey Royal' fame (only when grown there), this has kidney-shaped tubers with a waxy texture.
'Kestrel' – True potato-shaped, off-white tubers with purple rims around eyes. A good all-purpose variety; fair disease resistance.

MAINCROP

'Golden Wonder' – A late maincrop – harvest it after other maincrops. It has red-brown skin and a superb flavour that improves with age. Best for baking, roasting and frying.
'King Edward' – Old favourite with red-variegated tubers, known for its superb flavour, with cream-coloured flesh. Good for roasting and baking, but needs good growing conditions to do well.
'Mayan Gold' – Long, slender golden tubers with firm, golden, nutty-flavoured flesh. Great deep-fried whole or roasted; breaks up when boiled.

Exercise restraint

Unless you have a vast vegetable garden, or an allotment, and the storage capacity to match, it is far wiser to concentrate on growing some tasty earlies (new potatoes) and second earlies, than maincrop potatoes which are inexpensive to buy in the shops. New potatoes have an unbeatable flavour and texture when cooked soon after digging up. If you want to grow maincrop potatoes, pick one or two varieties that you won't get in the shops, such as 'Pink Fir Apple'. If you need more inspiration there are fascinating websites dedicated to potatoes of all kinds, including 'heritage' types.

'Picasso' – White-skinned potato decorated with splashes of pink. Cream-coloured tasty flesh. Good for all uses.
'Pink Fir Apple' – An old variety that makes the most fabulous potato salad and is also great baked, if you like a crispy skin. A very late maincrop with long, slim, knobbly tubers, best left in the ground until late autumn. Stores well right through winter.

Extra-early new potatoes under cover

For really early potatoes, buy seed potatoes as early as possible (midwinter, ideally) and chit them immediately (see box, page 102). When the shoots are 6mm (¼in) high, wait for a spell of mild weather (around early spring) and plant three tubers 13cm (5in) deep in a 40cm (15in) pot filled with a half-and-half mixture of John Innes No. 3 potting compost and multi-purpose compost, or plant six in a growbag and keep it in a frost-free greenhouse or conservatory with plenty of light. Once all risk of frost is past, the container can be moved outside, but for the very earliest crops,

Easily the most popular salad and new potato, 'International Kidney' (the name derived from its distinctive shape) is better known as 'Jersey Royal' when imported from that Channel Island.

continue growing them under cover. You could be picking your first new spuds by late spring.

'Mimi' is compact and good for growing like this; other potatoes grown in containers need stem support – the sort sold for supporting bushy herbaceous plants are ideal.

Enjoy them…

From early summer (first earlies), midsummer (second earlies) and autumn (maincrops). Use a fork carefully to dig up each plant individually, pushing the tines in 30cm (12in) or so away from the base and loosen the soil. Take a handful of stems at the base and gently pull – a lot of the potatoes will come up with the roots. Sift through the soil for the rest. Dig up second earlies in the same way.

Earlies often produce enough fair-sized tubers for a meal, even before the plants start to flower (flowering is a good indication that the crop is ready). Use your fingers to pull a few out without disturbing the plants, which will continue to grow.

Maincrops keep quite well in the soil even after the haulm (foliage) has died down, but need lifting before the weather turns wet to prevent attack by black keeled slugs. They may also start to grow again, which affects their keeping qualities.

Look out for…

Tubers affected by scab (irregular corky patches on the skin) look unattractive but are still edible – peeled. The disease is more prevalent on light soil that dries out badly in summer, especially on chalky ground, so adding plenty of organic matter a season before planting does help.

Potato blight is the most serious potato disease. Outbreaks are most likely during a wet summer; affected plants develop brown patches on the leaves (in damp conditions you'll also see white fungal rings around the brown spots on the backs of the leaves) in late summer and the foliage very quickly yellows and dies off. Early potatoes are rarely affected, since the tubers have usually been lifted before blight strikes, but if midsummer is rainy, start spraying plants with Bordeaux mixture to prevent the disease. Once it gets hold there's no cure. Dig up affected crops straight away and use tubers that are sound. Destroy the remains of affected plants; do not compost them.

Several different viruses affect potatoes: the edges of the leaves roll inwards, or leaves may develop yellow mosaic patterns. Viruses are often spread by aphids feeding on the leaves, but often occur when people save their own tubers to replant instead of buying seed potatoes. Affected plants are stunted with low yields.

It is best not to try to peel a 'Pink Fir Apple', but they taste just as good with the skin on.

There is nothing like harvesting potatoes to bring out the big kid in you. It's like striking oil.

Radishes

Summer radish
SOW MAR, APR, MAY, JUN, JUL, AUG
harvest MAY, JUN, JUL, AUG, SEP

Winter radish (including Chinese, Japanese, Mooli)
SOW JUL
harvest AUG, SEP, OCT, NOV

Radishes are the traditional accompaniment to a typical English salad, but can do so much more besides in stir fries and as crudités. They are a very quick crop – the quickest in fact, but this doesn't make them all that easy to grow. There are also oriental and winter radishes with large roots ready to pull in autumn and winter – they are worth trying for a change.

Cultivation
DIFFICULTY Easy; average input to provide what they need.
SOW In situ in succession throughout the growing season.
SPACE Thin summer radish seedlings to 2.5cm (1in) apart; allow 15cm (6in) between rows. Thin winter radishes to 5–7.5cm (2–3in) apart with 30cm (12in) between rows.
CARE Keep plants watered and well weeded. Thin out seedlings early.
YIELD As many as you like to sow.
STORAGE Summer ones are best eaten the day they are pulled, but will keep for a few days in the fridge. Winter ones can be stored for a short while in a cool dry place.

Keep them happy by…
Planting them in good, rich, well-drained fertile soil; but not anywhere that's recently had organic matter dug in or roots may split or fork.

Worth trying…
'French Breakfast' – Traditional cylindrical summer radish; red with a small white area at the base; very reliable.
'Mantanghong' or 'Beauty Heart' – Chinese winter radish; huge, tennis-ball-sized with green rind over red flesh. Crisp and sweet; make good 'vegetable crisps' or crudités.
'Mirabeau' – Long thin radishes with the traditional pink and white colouring; suitable for early sowing under cover as well as outdoors.
Mooli – Various types of Japanese winter radish with often

These 'French Breakfast' radish can be sown straight into the ground from early spring until mid-summer and will be ready for harvest in three to four weeks.

huge, hot-tasting, long, tapering to cylindrical white roots; used in oriental cookery.
'Scarlet Globe' – Popular, traditional, round, cherry-red summer radish; can be sown early/late under cover for out-of-season crops.

Enjoy them…
As soon as the first summer radish reaches useable size. Don't delay – they grow fast and then turn tough and woody, or bolt. From late summer if they are winter radishes. You'll have to dig, not pull, them up. Any left in the ground by late autumn should be dug up and stored in a dry, frost-free shed. Mooli varieties keep quite well until midwinter.

Look out for…
Poor soil, hot or dry conditions can all cause bolting.
Overcrowding or leaving it too late before thinning out seedlings will prevent roots developing freely.
Flea beetle can attack (*see* lettuce, page 94); a severe attack can kill small seedlings but is unlikely to harm bigger plants.

Shallots

plant FEB, MAR
harvest JUL, AUG

No longer grown simply for sloshing about in vinegar, shallots are now considered superior versions of onions. They have a more delicate appearance and lovely mild flavour and are as easy as onions to grow, with fewer problems. No reason not to pickle them still, though, if you prefer. Like onions, you buy them as sets; each set produces a cluster of offsets.

Cultivation

DIFFICULTY Easy; little input.
PLANT with a trowel, just covering them with soil.
SPACE 20cm (8in) apart in rows 30cm (12in) apart.
CARE Weed frequently and water in prolonged dry spells.
YIELD Up to 1.8kg (4lb) from a 1.5m (5ft) row.
STORAGE Spread them in shallow trays in a frost-proof shed or garage, or hang them up in a net in the shed roof; they'll last through winter.

Keep them happy by…

Planting the sets out of sight, under the soil. If they get pulled up shortly after planting, birds are the culprits. Replant them so that the tops are just covered this time. The problem stops when the shallots start taking root.

Worth trying…

'Golden Gourmet' – Large, golden-brown bulbs. Good flavour and a good keeper.
'Hative de Niort' – Very neat, small, globular, identical shallots popular for showing; not a very heavy cropper and can be difficult to find as sets.
'Jermor' – Tall, lean, upright shallots. Coppery skins and pink-tinged flesh; superb flavour.
'Prisma' – New variety; disease resistant with red skin and white flesh.
'Red Sun' – Rounded bulbs with rich, red-brown skin; good flavour and a long keeper.

Whereas with onions the single set, or bulb, grows bigger, with shallots it splits to produce a number of offsets.

Enjoy them…

After the leaves have turned yellow naturally in late summer. Lift clumps carefully with a fork, shake off the soil and put them on the ground to dry off in the sun before storing.

Look out for…

Poor growing conditions can cause crop failure or small offsets. This could be due to poor infertile soil, cold wet weather or lack of water. Have you been a good weeder? Shallots, like all onions, hate competition from weeds.

Onions growing with shallots in a well-tended vegetable bed.

Spinach

Summer spinach
SOW MAR, APR, MAY
harvest MAY, JUN, JUL, AUG, SEP

Autumn spinach
SOW AUG, SEP, OCT
harvest SEP, OCT, NOV

Spinach is so convenient to buy in neat bags, ready washed, but it is also pretty easy to grow and you can have it much cheaper and fresher that way, still bursting with health-giving nutrients. Most of the modern varieties are dual-purpose: you can eat them raw in salads when the leaves are tiny and then cooked when they're bigger.

Cultivation

DIFFICULTY Easy; low input.
SOW Thinly in rows in situ, or scatter in large tubs or in an intensive salad bed. If you want baby salad leaves, sow every 4–6 weeks during the sowing season. (Note: not all seeds are suitable for sowing in autumn; check the packet.)
SPACE By thinning to 2.5cm (1in) apart for baby leaves, or

7.5cm (3in) for cooking-size leaves – use thinnings in salads.
CARE Water and weed assiduously. It's essential for the plants to grow steadily without a check. Seeds sown in early summer are less likely to succeed as the summer months are too hot and the soil too dry for most spinach varieties; if they do grow they are likely to bolt. Grow other salad leaves (see pages 94–6) during the height of summer.
YIELD Up to 2.3kg (5lb) from a 1.5m (5ft) row.
STORAGE Best eaten just-picked, but will keep for a couple of days in the fridge and can be frozen (see Storage, pages 58–9).

Keep them happy by...
Providing rich, fertile soil containing enough nitrogen.

Worth trying...
'Bordeaux' – Bright red leaf stalks and leaf veins make this ideal for baby salad leaves. Can also be sown in late winter and from late summer to autumn.
'Galaxy' – Mildew-resistant variety for baby leaves. Can be grown through the winter under cover, even on a bright windowsill.
'Medania' – All-round variety for sowing in spring or summer to produce 'baby' spinach leaves, also in autumn to grow under cover for cutting the following spring.

Enjoy them...
As baby leaves as soon as they are big enough to use, usually within a month of sowing. Cut the crop little and often. For cooking, start cutting leaves when the plants reach a suitable size (6–8 weeks after sowing) – don't wait too long or they will bolt and the leaves won't be so tasty.

Look out for...
Downy mildew can affect crops, especially those under cover, particularly in cold, dull, humid weather; modern disease-resistant varieties fend off all but the worst attacks.

Bolting is triggered by high temperatures, shortage of water or poor soil with insufficient organic matter, but spinach plants are not long-lived anyway and all run to seed eventually. Sow frequently for a continuous supply.

The leaves of spinach 'Bordeaux' are coloured by rich red stalks and veins, which makes them pretty in the garden as well as tasty on the plate.

Perpetual spinach

SOW APR, MAY, JUN, JUL
harvest JUL, AUG, SEP, OCT

Perpetual spinach is excellent for providing you with a spinachy vegetable nearly all year round. It is less fragile than 'real' spinach, the same plants are easily capable of surviving the hotter summer months and on through winter in milder areas. In flavour and texture, it's very much like Swiss chard, but without the thick midribs. Only one variety is usually available.

Winter crops

Remember to sow a row or two of perpetual spinach in midsummer under cover. The resulting plants will stay in perfect condition through the winter and start growing again in spring, producing enormous crops of large, tender, unblemished leaves until they run to seed in late spring.

Alternatively, sow perpetual spinach seed outdoors in midsummer and protect the plants with fleece over winter (*see page 39*). They can survive the cold without protection, but the leaves will be battered and unfit to use.

Cultivation

DIFFICULTY Easy; little input.
SOW thinly in rows where you want the plants to crop.
SPACE seedlings by thinning to 15cm (6in) apart with 30cm (12in) between rows.
CARE Keep plants watered in dry spells and weed regularly.
YIELD Up to 2.3kg (5lb) from a 1.5m (5ft) row.
STORAGE Best eaten just-picked, but will keep for a couple of days in the fridge.

Enjoy them...

As soon as the leaves are big enough to use; don't over-pick plants – cut little and often from all over the row and allow plants to recover between times.

Look out for...

Slugs can be a nuisance, but this is really a trouble-free crop.

Perpetual spinach is more robust than 'real' spinach and the leaves are more shiny and a bit tougher – they don't cook down to such a pulp. The taste is also slightly different, but just as good.

New Zealand spinach

SOW APR, MAY, JUN
harvest JUN, JUL, AUG, SEP, OCT

The shoots of New Zealand spinach are excellent steamed, but not for use raw in salads. It thrives in the hot conditions that 'normal' spinach hates. The same plants crop all summer right up to the first proper frost. Under cool cover the cropping season is slightly longer and the plants may self-seed, or you can collect the seed.

Sow the seed in a hot, sunny, sheltered spot with well-drained soil. Thin the seedlings to 15–20cm (6–8in) apart, with 45cm (18in) between rows. Water sparingly, if at all; keep well weeded until plants cover the ground, when no weeds will be able to grow.

Start picking as soon as plants are a just a few inches high; cut or snap off tips of shoots about 2.5–5cm (1–2in) long. Pick little and often, at least two or three times a week to keep plants productive – that is, bushy and leafy.

Squashes and pumpkins

SOW APR **plant** MAY, JUN
harvest OCT

Squashes and pumpkins make huge plants and need plenty of room – and they don't repay the space with quantity, it must be admitted – but they are easy to grow and kids love them. While they can be good for soup, pumpkins are usually more popular for making Halloween lanterns, while squashes tend to be more versatile and are great roasted or added to seasonal autumn stews and pies. (For summer squashes, *see* under courgettes, page 84).

Squashes are renowned for their odd shapes, and few are odder than the aptly named 'Turk's Turban' – bright orange, streaked with cream and green; best roasted for its roast-chestnut flavour.

Cultivation

DIFFICULTY Easy; low input after good soil preparation.

SOW singly in pots on a windowsill indoors or in a heated propagator in the greenhouse at 18–24°C (65–75°F). Grow on at 13–18°C (55–65°F) – a cool room or shaded, sheltered cold frame is ideal.

PLANT Harden off and plant when the last frosts are safely past, from late spring. After planting, surround each plant with a ring of soil, about 30cm (12in) from the stem; fill this with water each time you water.

SPACE 90cm (3ft) apart.

CARE Water sparingly at first. As the plants get going, water regularly to keep the soil moist and feed with liquid fertilizer. Weed until the plants cover the ground and smother the competition. Slowly reduce the feeding and watering towards the end of summer to encourage the fruit to start ripening, and as early autumn arrives, carefully remove foliage overshadowing the fruits to allow the sun to reach them and develop their full colour.

YIELD Three fruits per plant.

STORAGE Allow the fruits to dry in the sun, turning them over so the underneath can dry too. Store them in a dry, frost-free shed or garage where they should keep for several months; alternatively, bring them indoors to a dry, coolish room.

Keep them happy by…

Planting them in very rich, very well-manured soil or dig a large hole in autumn and spend winter filling it with materials you'd usually put on the compost heap. In spring, cover it with a mound of soil and plant there. You can even grow them on the compost heap – put a few inches of soil on top first.

Worth trying…

'Avalon' and 'Harrier' – versions of the butternut squash (the light-bulb-shaped, beige squash that greengrocers sell). The true butternut is unlikely to ripen even in a good summer, but these have been bred for our weather conditions.

'Becky' – The ideal Halloween pumpkin.

'Crown Prince' – Medium-sized, squat, steely blue-grey pumpkins with orange flesh; good for roasting and pumpkin soup.

'Hasta La Pasta' – Long, bright orange, marrow-like squashes; it yields 'vegetable spaghetti', obtained by baking whole then removing the shredded flesh in the centre using a fork.

'Sweet Dumpling' – Small, green-striped, cream squashes produced at the rate of 4–6 per plant. Delicious baked and stuffed whole or sliced and roasted.

Enjoy them...

Once they are ripe; allow them to grow to full size on the plant then cut them carefully, leaving a short length of stem. Pick them all up off the ground by mid-autumn, before sitting on cold, damp ground causes rotting on the undersides of the skins.

Look out for...

Mosaic virus (*see* courgettes, page 84) can affect pumpkins and squashes – look out for yellow mottling on the leaves and poor growth. Pull out and destroy affected plants.

Mice and larger rodents may nibble the skins of pumpkins, especially before they ripen and harden; make sure your compost heaps are not home to such wildlife before planting in them.

Slugs may damage young fruits while the skins are very soft, and damaged areas deform as the fruits grow larger. It's not usually a problem unless you want a perfect specimen for showing; deep wounds may allow in fungal organisms, which cause rot in a damp season.

In a good year you can have many more pumpkins and squashes than you can eat, but they store well and are very decorative.

Growing a monster

Choose the right variety, such as 'Atlantic Giant', 'Big Max', 'Dill's Giant Atlantic', 'Hundredweight', 'Sumo Giant'.

Start plants and harden off as normal. Plant using the pit-full-of compost method. After planting, cover the plant with a cloche or fleece for protection (uncover it on fine days), until it grows too big or the weather really warms up.

Allow three fruits to set and start to swell, then select the largest and remove all the rest. This means the plant directs all its energies into just the one fruit. Weed, water and feed as normal. If you are really keen, bury the trailing stems in very good soil, only just covering them. They will grow roots to help feed your monster pumpkin.

To improve your chances and choice, grow several plants, spaced 2–3m (6–10ft) apart.

'Atlantic Giant' is capable of growing to enormous proportions.

Swedes

SOW MAY, JUN
harvest JAN, FEB AND SEP, OCT, NOV, DEC

Perhaps because it is cheap and not very pretty, the poor old swede has a reputation for being staid and boring, but mashed with carrots or potato and with some butter and pepper added, it is a great comfort food. Perhaps it would be more popular if we called it by its more exotic American name of rutabaga?

Cultivation

DIFFICULTY Easy; little input.

SOW seeds thinly in situ in early summer – timing is critical.

SPACE seedlings by thinning in several stages until they are 23cm (9in) apart, allow 40cm (15in) between rows.

CARE Hoe regularly and water well in dry weather – keep the soil evenly moist, as wide fluctuations between wet and dry conditions can cause the roots to split and spoil.

YIELD Up to 6.8kg (15lb) from a 1.5m (5ft) row.

STORAGE They keep best in the ground until needed, but dig them up if your garden is on heavy clay or if prolonged freezing temperatures are forecast.

Keep them happy by...

Giving them an open, airy situation in full sun; don't grow them crowded together or overshadowed by surrounding crops.

Worth trying...

'Brora' – A new variety with excellent flavour, purple skin and yellow flesh.

'Invitation' – Modern variety with purple-flushed skin, bred for resistance to clubroot and mildew.

'Marian' – The traditional flavoursome variety with purple tops and yellow-cream bases; very resistant to mildew and clubroot.

Enjoy them...

Towards autumn when the roots become big enough to use; you don't have to wait until they are the size of the ones in the shops. Pull individuals as you want them and leave the rest to continue growing.

Look out for...

They can suffer clubroot like all brassicas (*see* page 74). Choose a resistant variety.

Powdery mildew can also be a problem; again the answer is in your choice of variety.

The swede is long overdue for a comeback – it's a tasty, hearty root vegetable that's also pretty easy to grow and a great addition to winter soups and stews.

Sweetcorn

SOW APR plant MAY, JUN
harvest JUL, AUG, SEP

For true fans, the only way to eat sweetcorn is picked fresh from your own crop and cooked minutes later. The sugars start to turn to starch as soon as the cob is removed from its parent, so every minute counts. If you find frozen or tinned sweetcorn too sweet it could be that you are eating the supersweet varieties; try growing a 'normal' variety – you may find it more to your taste.

Cultivation

DIFFICULTY Easy to intermediate; lowish input.
SOW one seed per small pot on a windowsill or in a heated propagator at 16–21°C (60–70°F) in spring. Grow on in slightly cooler temperatures. Harden off for planting out when the frosts are over, in early summer.
PLANT sweetcorn in blocks not rows, as the plants are wind-pollinated and this is the best way of ensuring good pollination.
SPACE 45cm (18in) apart in each direction.
CARE Cover young plants with fleece (see page 39) on cold nights to help them establish quickly. Water in dry spells. No support is needed, even though the plants grow quite tall.
YIELD Two cobs per plant.
STORAGE Eat as soon as picked, or freeze as soon as picked.

Keep them happy by...

Planting them slightly deeper than the soil level in the pot. This encourages tillering – putting out small side shoots and more roots – and makes the plants more stable.

Worth trying...

'Applause' – Supersweet F1 new(ish)comer.
'Incredible' – Sugar-enhanced, reliable variety; ripens mid-season.
'Minipop' – For baby corn cobs 10–15cm (4–6in) long; plant all baby varieties only 20cm (8in) apart and pick before pollination (the tassels are still silky and pale).

Modern varieties of sweetcorn, such as 'Golden Bantam' are bred for reliability in our unreliable climate. They are late-ripening, so good for extending the cropping season when grown with an earlier one, such as 'Sundance'.

'Sundance' – 'Normal' F1 variety with 18cm (7in) cobs; matures early and crops reliably, even in poor summers.

Enjoy them...

As soon as the cobs ripen in late summer. You can tell they are ripe as the silky tassels turn brown and dry up, but you should double-check by testing the cobs too: peel back a little of the leaf-like green sheath to expose a few kernels and press a thumbnail into one or two – if clear liquid spurts out the cob is not quite ripe; when it's ready to pick the juice is milky.

Look out for...

Poor pollination can mean that you have gappy cobs – areas without kernels. They are still edible.

Fruit fly larvae distort the developing tips of young plants so that they grow stunted and twisted and produce unusable, underdeveloped cobs. Protect young plants with insect-proof mesh (see page 52) and pull out and destroy affected plants.

Swiss chard

SOW APR, MAY, JUN, JUL
harvest JUL, AUG, SEP, OCT

Swiss chard is a great green vegetable, like a mild
spinach but with more substance – it doesn't cook down
to mush. As well as being quite tasty, it looks attractive in
the garden with its big shiny leaves and white leaf stalks.
There are also varieties with orange or pink leaf stalks
and leaf veins and these look wonderful with the
morning or evening sun shining through them.

Cultivation

DIFFICULTY Easy; little input.
SOW in mid-spring to midsummer in rows outside.
SPACE 15cm (6in) apart with 30cm (12in) between rows.
CARE Keep plants watered in dry spells and weed regularly.
YIELD 1.4kg (3lb) from a 1.5m (5ft) row.
STORAGE Pick and use fresh rather than store.

Worth trying …

'Bright Lights' – A mixture of red-, white- and yellow-stemmed
varieties; its decorative qualities are its main asset. The
thinnings can be used to brighten salads.
Ruby chard – Slender bright red stems and purple-tinged dark
green leaves; it is not quite such a strong grower as Swiss chard,
so grow it if you want decoration as well as food.

Keep them happy by…

Doing next to nothing; they are very easy to please.

Enjoy them…

As soon as individual chard leaves are big enough to use,
around midsummer from early sowings. Use a sharp knife to
cut through the stem at the base of the plant, taking care
not to slice into neighbouring stems. Early-sown chard plants
are usually finished by the autumn, but midsummer-sown
crops often withstand a mild winter. If there's a really cold
spell they may die down, but regrow in spring to produce a
short-lived crop of tender leaves before running to seed in
late spring. The leaves can be steamed or cooked like
spinach; the leaf stalks boiled like celery, but most folk stick
to cooking just the leaves since the flavour of the stalk is
nothing to write home about!

'Fordhook Giant' has long, thick, white, flattened and ribbed
stems with glossy, crinkled, dark green leaves; connoisseurs
are sure that the flavour is better than that of the coloured
varieties. It reaches the large size of 55–68cm (22–27in) tall
and 30cm (12in) across.

Look out for…

Snails can make a meal of them, but they often prefer to hide in
the bigger leaves, which you won't want to eat anyway. Check
them carefully when you wash them before cooking. Otherwise
this is a trouble-free crop.

Tomatoes

Indoor
SOW FEB, MAR **plant** APR, MAY
harvest JUL, AUG, SEP, OCT

Outdoor
SOW MAR **plant** MAY, JUN
harvest JUL, AUG, SEP, OCT

Cherry, plum and giant beefsteak, yellow, brown, white and striped – you could eat a different tomato on almost every day of the year, so great and wide is the choice. They are not the most accommodating of plants, though, being quite demanding and prone to almost as many problems as there are varieties, but even if you experience difficulties one year, you're sure to succeed the next. In the end, home-grown tomatoes are worth it.

Cultivation

DIFFICULTY Intermediate; they crave attention – don't turn your back on them.

SOW seeds on a windowsill indoors or in a heated propagator at 18–21°C (65–70°F) from late winter to early spring for plants for growing in an unheated greenhouse, or mid-spring for growing outside. You can sow a little bit later if you live in a cold area; it makes no sense to have plants that are 60cm (24in) tall at planting time – 30cm (12in) is better.

PLANT in the greenhouse (in soil borders or pots) from mid- to late spring, avoiding cold spells. Plant outdoors after the last frost is safely past, usually late spring to early summer.

SPACE 60cm (24in) apart in borders under cover; outside plant them 75cm (2½ft) apart with 90cm (3ft) between rows.

CARE You'll need to support the plants and feed, water, tie up and trim them regularly. Anticipate spending a bit of time on caring for your tomato plants every week on top of routine watering (*see* box on page 116 for specifics).

YIELD Varies with the type.

STORAGE Eat fresh, or make into sauces to freeze (*see* Storage, pages 58–9).

Worth trying...

'Ailsa Craig' – Traditional and popular cordon for outside or under cover; medium-sized round, red fruits. Often available as young plants at garden centres at planting time.

'Brandywine' – US beefsteak cordon variety for under cover; large pink fruits with outstanding flavour and potato-like leaves.

'Gardener's Delight' – Hugely and deservedly popular cordon for outdoors or under cover; huge trusses of sweet, cherry-sized tomatoes are among the first to start ripening.

'Green Grape' – Cordon best grown under cover or on a very warm and sheltered patio; bite-sized green fruits ripen from jade green to yellowy, lime green; exceptionally sweet and mild, almost like a real grape.

'Ildi' – Cordon for under cover or outside; bunches literally dripping with small, sweet, teardrop-shaped, yellow fruit that ripen in succession – almost too many to eat.

'Marmande' – A French beefsteak cordon with lobed, red fruits for growing outside; 'stop' the plants (remove the tops of the

If you have a penchant for really big 'meaty' tomatoes, you can't go far wrong with 'Brandywine', but you do need to grow it in a greenhouse or polytunnel.

main stems) after two or three flower trusses have set fruit, as they can't support a huge crop.

'Roma' – Bushy variety reaching waist-high for indoors or outside; flavoursome and nicely shaped, red plum tomatoes, lots of juice and few seeds.

'Sungold' – Cordon for outdoors or under cover; lots of small orange-yellow cherry tomatoes of superb flavour.

'Tigerella' – Cordon best under cover; striking large, striped fruit with a tangy taste; the fruit are light and dark green at first, ripening to orange-yellow then to red with orange stripes.

'Tornado' – Outdoor bush variety that does well even in a poor summer, with very well-flavoured, medium, round, red fruits.

'Tumbler' – Compact, trailing, easy-to-grow bush tomato, ideal for hanging baskets, window boxes or tall containers; it produces a modest crop of small, round, red tomatoes.

Enjoy them…

Straight from the plants when they have ripened fully. Indoors this can be from midsummer, outdoors from late summer. If you aren't going to eat them straight away, snip them off just above the green calyx to help them keep better. In a good season, plants will continue to ripen fruit until late autumn under cover, early autumn outdoors.

In late summer, start removing new flowers (they'll never fruit) and remove the growing tip (or tips, in bush varieties). Reduce the amount of watering drastically. Remove a few of the lower leaves, especially those that are already yellowing, to allow more light and air to circulate.

When you want to clear the plants, remove any full-sized green tomatoes and put them in a dark place indoors. Don't put them on a sunny windowsill – this makes them shrivel up without ripening. You could put them in a box with a ripe apple or banana, since the fruit gives off ethylene gas, which hastens maturity – though not flavour, but it's better than nothing.

Look out for…

Tomatoes suffer from many ailments.

Soil-borne diseases build up when they are regularly grown in the same soil. Eventually your crop will hardly be worth having. Problems are more common in soil borders under cover and can be rectified by digging out and replacing the soil as far as possible or using growing bags or pots instead.

Split fruit occurs as result of stress, caused when plants are alternately wet and dry at the roots. Avoid it by watering little

It's always so tempting to try different tomato varieties – there are so many of them – but in the end, among the cherries, 'Gardener's Delight' always comes out near the top.

and often. It's common on outdoor plants during a dry summer when there's suddenly lots of rain. Pick affected fruits – they're usually the riper ones anyway – and purée them so they don't go to waste.

Blossom end rot is a sunken, black leathery patch on the base (or blossom end) of the tomato. It is most common in container plants – especially those in growing bags – and is due to the plants occasionally being allowed to dry out. To prevent it, water regularly. Plants grown in the ground are rarely affected. Outdoor tomatoes are susceptible to potato blight (*see* page 104). Keep a close watch for early symptoms (brown patches on the leaves), particularly if there is rain in early and midsummer, and, as with potatoes, spray outdoor tomatoes with Bordeaux mixture as a precaution. Repeat every fortnight and you may save the crop. Once leaves start looking dead and both ripe and unripe fruit develop brown, rotten-looking patches, it's too late. Tomatoes grown under cover are less likely to be affected but they aren't totally immune, since the spores can enter through ventilators and doors. A few blight-resistant varieties are starting to become available.

Botrytis affects different parts of tomato plants in different ways: fluffy, grey sunken patches on stems, grey mouldy flowers that drop off without setting fruit, small, round, translucent 'ghost spots' on the skin of green tomatoes. It's more of a problem under cover; avoid it by ventilating more and limiting watering to the base of the plants to avoid excess humidity in the air. In a particularly bad case, use a suitable fungicide.

Whitefly are little white flies that live on the undersides of the leaves and fly out when you tap the plant. They suck sap and secrete sticky honeydew, which may then grow sooty mould. They are difficult to control as the young are tough and scale-like. Use a biological control (*see* page 53) under glass. They're less of a problem outdoors, but if you have had an attack last year grow companion plants (*see* Companion planting, page 52); fuzzy-leaved marigolds, *Tagetes minuta*, grown alongside the tomato plants will help deter them. Sticky traps can be effective, but they can also catch beneficial insects.

'Tigerella' has a slightly tangy flavour and its colour really makes a difference in salads.

Keeping them happy

PLANTING
You are almost always going to get a better crop from plants grown under cover, but it is worth having a few plants outdoors in a sunny sheltered spot.

In a greenhouse, plant into a soil border that's been well prepared or use pots 40cm (15in) in diameter and filled with a mixture of John Innes No. 2 potting compost and multipurpose compost (half and half). In the ground outside, plant tomatoes in a warm sheltered spot and give them slightly more room (*see* Cultivation notes). Growing bags are another choice, either under cover or outdoors, but limit yourself to two plants in each one and do take extra care with the watering – it can be difficult to get right.

WATERING
Immediately after planting, give each plant ½ litre (1 pint) of water, then let it go slightly short of water until the first flowers open. Gradually increase watering when the green fruits start to swell. Container-grown plants carrying a crop of ripening fruits need watering once or twice daily; those in the ground can make do with every few days. Into the soil beside each plant, sink a 10cm (4in) plastic flowerpot or an upside-down plastic bottle with the bottom cut off, pour the water into this so that the water goes straight to the roots.

FEEDING
Start feeding with liquid tomato feed while the young plants are still in their pots, prior to planting out. After planting, feed once a week, make this twice a week once they start carrying a crop.

SUPPORTING AND TRAINING
Cordon (single-stemmed varieties) need a single cane. Bush varieties do better with three shorter canes to support their bushier shape. Tie the main stems to the canes to stop them being weighed down by the developing crop and breaking. Tie in new growth every week. With cordon tomatoes, remove all the sideshoots that grow in the angle where each leaf joins the main stem. This needs doing every week. Bush tomatoes don't need their sideshoots removed; if they grow too big and bushy, however, you could thin out the growth a bit.

Turnips

Under cover
SOW MAR AND AUG, SEP
harvest MAY, JUN AND OCT, NOV

Outdoors
SOW APR, MAY, JUN, JUL
harvest JUN, JUL, AUG, SEP

As far as baby vegetables go, it is hard to beat turnips. At this size they are still tender and have a wonderful flavour, not to mention a range of interesting colours that look great on the plate. You can eat them raw when they are young, too, and if you do let them grow a bit big, you can always stew or bake them with other veg for what nowadays is an unusual treat.

Like swedes, turnips have a reputation for being staid in the taste department, but that's only because the ones we remember eating were probably months old before they reached our plate. Fresh home-grown turnip is something altogether different.

Cultivation

DIFFICULTY Easy; low input.
SOW Early under cover, later outdoors, thinly in situ.
SPACE 2.5cm (1in) apart for baby veg; 5cm (2in) apart for normal crops. Allow 15–20cm (6–8in) between rows.
CARE Water regularly and keep well weeded to avoid competition and to ensure the plants grow steadily without a check, otherwise they tend to become fibrous and tough.
YIELD 1.4–1.8kg (3–4lb) from a 1.5m (5ft) row.
STORAGE They keep for a few days in the fridge.

Keep them happy by…

Remembering that they are a member of the brassica family and need to be given similar growing conditions: especially well-prepared firm ground.

Worth trying…

'Atlantic' – Traditional-looking, reliable turnip, like a flattened ball with a purple top; good for sowing early and late under cover, as well as outdoors. Known to the French as 'navets'.
'Golden Ball' – A round turnip with flavoursome golden flesh; grow outdoors.
'Snowball' – Long-established turnip with sweet white flesh.
'Tokyo Cross' – If you can find it, it is great for sowing under cover. Produces its pure white little balls of flavour in six weeks.

Enjoy them…

When they are almost 2.5cm (1in) across. Pull them up gently. Turnips more than 5cm (2in) across are too fibrous and lacking in flavour, by this stage they are only fit for the chickens.

Look out for…

It is a brassica and prey to clubroot (*see* page 74). There are currently no resistant varieties.

Turnip gall weevil is caused by a larva living inside the root, which it hollows out, causing distortion that looks similar to clubroot. Cut a root open: if it's gall weevil you'll find the tunnel; if it's clubroot the flesh will stink. Gall weevil isn't a problem – just throw away affected roots.

Flea beetle likes turnips and will sprinkle leaves with tiny round holes. Use insect-proof mesh, tucked in well around the plants (*see* page 52), to protect turnip crops as a severe infestation will check their growth underground, which you don't want at all.

A–Z of Herbs

It may seem like a bit of a cliché, but no vegetable garden is complete without a selection of culinary herbs, and once you start cooking with your own home-grown vegetables it is a natural step to grow your own herbs to accompany them.

Herbs to grow

Herb plants are available from garden centres and supermarkets but it is also well worth a visit to a herb farm, where the proprietors will be able to provide you with lots of advice about growing, storing and using these plants. Start out with a few tried-and-tested favourites and then expand your herb collection as you expand your repertoire of recipes. Remember, too, that many herbs don't like the rich, moisture-retentive growing conditions that you have created in your vegetable patch, so provide them with what they need.

Basil

SOW MAY, JUN
plant JUN, JUL, AUG
harvest JUN, JUL, AUG, SEP, OCT

Basil is among the most popular culinary herbs. Its soft, bright green leaves and wonderful clove scent make it a great addition to the vegetable garden or kitchen windowsill. It is slow growing from seed, but the intense flavour of home-raised basil leaves is worth the wait.

Cultivation

DIFFICULTY Intermediate; it needs above average input.
SOW and plant in pots on windowsills indoors at room temperature all year round, or in a greenhouse or conservatory in summer. Thin out very overcrowded seedlings, but allow several young plants to grow in the same pot to make a bushy 'plant'.
PLANT these potfuls outside in a container filled with multipurpose compost, or plant them in the ground in a warm, sheltered sunny spot in well-drained humus-rich soil.
SPACE Individual potfuls about 15cm (6in) apart.
CARE Water sparingly, little and often; use a general-purpose liquid feed regularly on container plants to encourage them to remain leafy. As soon as flower buds appear at the tips of the shoots, nip them off to encourage further leafy growth.
STORAGE Basil can be dried, but its flavour is never as good.

Keep it happy by...

Giving the seedlings warmth; seeds started indoors are more likely to succeed. The plants also like plenty of sun and fertile soil. Sow new plants every month or so, to maintain supplies.

Worth trying...

'Genovese' – A cultivar renowned for its fragrance and the traditional basil for pesto, but a good all-rounder as well.
Bush basil – A compact, dome-shaped bush with small leaves.

The most commonly grown basil is 'Genovese' – it's the one sold in supermarkets. It has shiny, soft leaves that are bursting with a clean clove and mint taste.

'Ararat' – This variety has green leaves flecked with purple.
'Kemangie' – This is also called lemon basil and combines basil and lemon flavouring.
'Neapolitana' – This variety has very large crinkled leaves with a good strong flavour.
'Purple Ruffles' – The chief attraction of this basil is its extravagantly ruffled, rich purple leaves.

Enjoy it...

Start picking little and often as soon as the leaves are big enough to use. Don't remove whole shoots as this will set the plants back.

Look out for...

The seedlings are prone to damping off and young plants may develop black stem bases due to cold or damp conditions.

Greenfly is common, especially on indoor plants. Move plants grown in pots outside in summer to improve ventilation and to enable natural predators to do their bit. Avoid using pesticides as you are going to eat the leaves!

Bay

plant MAY, JUN, JUL
harvest YEAR ROUND

Bay is a versatile herb that is used in any number of dishes, from stews and soups to marinades and sauces, and is a key ingredient in bouquet garni, along with parsley, thyme and other herbs. The leaves are tough so are usually removed before the food is served. The plant itself is an evergreen that is capable of growing into a large bushy tree in southern counties, but is usually seen trained as a smallish, globe- or cone-shaped shrub, often in a large container.

Cultivation

DIFFICULTY Easy; low input.
PLANT small specimens outside after the last frosts; they need good growing weather to become established before winter.
SPACE You are unlikely to need more than one bay plant. Give it plenty of space.
CARE Water and liquid-feed pot-grown plants throughout summer. In winter, bring trained pot plants into a greenhouse or sheltered corner of the garden; water sparingly if the compost dries out. Plants growing in open ground only need pruning and are otherwise self-sufficient. Use secateurs to prune the shape back into trained plants in mid-spring; remove whole leaves, don't cut into them.
STORAGE You won't need to store any as you can pick leaves fresh all year round.

Training a standard

You will need a single-stemmed plant. Push a cane into the pot or soil beside the stem and tie it in to keep the growth straight. Remove sideshoots until the plant reaches the top of the cane, then nip out the very tip of the plant to encourage sideshoots to develop all round the top. When they are 7.5–10cm (3–4in) long, remove tips to encourage them to branch. Continue doing this until you have a dense head of foliage. Prune in spring to maintain its shape; and again in late summer.

Sometimes called bay laurel, bay makes an attractive addition to the herb garden and keeps it leaves all year round.

Keep it happy by…

Growing it in a bright sunny spot and providing pot-grown plants with plenty of water and food in the growing season.

Worth trying…

Bay (*Laurus nobilis*) – Only this species is available. It has oval, dark, evergreen shiny leaves.

Enjoy it…

At any time of year. Choose undamaged, full-sized but young leaves for cooking.

Look out for…

Pot-grown specimens are particularly prone to scale insect attack. These browny yellow creatures attach themselves to the undersides of leaves, usually along the main veins. Their sticky secretions encourage sooty mould, which is unattractive and spreads quickly. Wash the leaves with a soft cloth or cotton wool ball wetted with soft soap or washing-up liquid (diluted as you would for washing up) to remove the pests and the mould.

Chives

plant APR, MAY, JUN, JUL
harvest MAY, JUN, JUL, AUG, SEP

Chives are among the best known of herbs. The mildly onion-flavoured leaves are hollow and tubular and wonderful chopped up in salads, particularly potato salad. They are one of the ingredients for *fines herbes*: the others are traditionally chervil, parsley and tarragon. The rounded heads of lavender-purple flowers appear in early summer, decorating the vegetable garden and attracting bees. Chive plants are perennial and can be lifted and divided at almost any time to increase your stocks. They may even gently self-seed.

Cultivation

DIFFICULTY Easy; virtually no input.
PLANT pot-grown clumps in late spring or summer.
SPACE Clumps about 15cm (6in) apart.
CARE Water in new plants and weed when necessary.
STORAGE They don't store unless dried, so pot up a clump and bring it indoors for use over winter.

Keep them happy by...

Watering during dry periods. You can remove the spent flowerheads by simply pulling gently on the flowering stem, which will come out neatly from the base of the plant. Do this as necessary through the summer.

Worth trying...

Chives (*Allium schoenoprasum*) – This is the only widely available form. Its rounded heads of flowers are 2.5cm (1in) across on 15cm (8in) stalks and held just above the tops of the plants. White chives (*Allium schoenoprasum* 'White Form') – White-flowered chives are rare but sometimes sold by herb nurseries. Garlic chives, Chinese chives (*Allium tuberosum*) – The flat, narrow leaves of this perennial species have a mild garlic flavour. The plants are taller than common chives, at 30cm (12in) high, and have clusters of white flowers at the top of the stems in summer.

Enjoy them...

As soon as the leaves are long enough to cut. Cut the leaves at their base, about 2.5cm (1in) above the ground, and take a few from each clump so that the appearance of the plant isn't spoiled.

Dig up and divide a clump of chives at the end of summer. Plant a couple of small clumps into small pots and replant the rest in the garden. Cut down the top growth in the potted clumps to 2.5cm (1in) and bring them indoors. They will respond by re-shooting, providing you with fresh leaves over winter.

Look out for...

Chives can grow spindly if overcrowded by other plants or if in too much shade. Move them into the light. Lanky plants with yellowing or broken and bent leaves can be cut down to 2.5–5cm (1–2in) above the ground and will soon make fresh new growth.

Chives produce generous quantities of small lavender-purple flowerheads, which are long lasting and beloved by bees.

Coriander

SOW MAY, JUN, JUL
harvest JUN, JUL, AUG, SEP

Coriander is well known for its deeply cut, aromatic leaves, which are added to soups, salads and all manner of other dishes, but its seeds are also invaluable and have a delicate but exotic spicy flavour. They are used in the subtle Indian spice mixture garam masala. There are coriander varieties bred specially for leaf production; they are well worth going for as they have a long season, otherwise you tend to get flowers and seeds far too quickly.

Cultivation

DIFFICULTY Intermediate; needs some special care.

SOW in rows or patio containers every six weeks or so from late spring until midsummer. You can also sow coriander on the kitchen windowsill to have fresh leaves all year round. To harvest coriander seed, you need to sow by May.

SPACE The seedlings of seed-bearing varieties 7.5–10cm (3–4in) apart, with 30cm (12in) between rows. With leaf coriander thin only if the plants are very overcrowded and use the thinnings in the kitchen.

CARE Water sparingly as seedlings may damp off if allowed to get too wet.

STORAGE Dry the seeds on a shallow tray then store them in screw-top glass jars in a cool, dark place. Grind them just before use for maximum flavour.

When well grown, coriander is a lush plant with delicate divided foliage.

Keep them happy by...

Making sure you weed around the plants. Coriander doesn't like being crowded and you are less likely to get a good crop of seeds if it is. And put them somewhere warm, sheltered and sunny – they won't thrive in cool conditions.

Worth trying...

FOR SEEDS 'Moroccan' and the species (*Coriandrum sativum*) – These will produce heads of tiny white flowers on stalks about 60cm (2ft) high, followed by seeds. 'Moroccan' is particularly fast to flower and set seed.

FOR LEAVES 'Cilantro' and 'Leisure' – These are leaf varieties of coriander and particularly good for later sowings. You can grow them as a cut-and-come-again crop, keeping them around 10cm (4in) tall.

Enjoy them...

As leaves as soon as they are big enough to use: the same plants should re-shoot several times if you are careful to leave at least 2.5–5cm (1–2in) of growth above the base of the plant.

For seeds it is best not to cut the leaves at all. The flowerheads start to produce green seeds towards the end of the summer. When these turn buff-brown, cut the stems and hang them upside down in a warm, airy place out of direct sun. Tie paper bags over the heads to catch any seeds that drop.

Look out for...

A cold wet summer can mean the plants struggle. In this case place pots of leaf coriander on an indoor windowsill. Seed coriander can be grown in the soil border of a greenhouse or polytunnel, but watch out for high humidity, which can cause fungal disease.

Dill

SOW APR, MAY, JUN
harvest MAY, JUN, JUL, AUG

This statuesque herb has pale green feathery leaves on tall stems and flat flowerheads like yellow cow-parsley. It is a decorative plant for a flower border as well as the corner of your veg garden. Dill has an aniseed taste and it is popularly used for baking and poaching fish, particularly salmon, but the feathery leaves can also be used as a garnish, like parsley, and their unique flavour is pleasant in green salads. They are also used in mustard sauces.

The leaves of dill are so feathery as to be hardly leaves at all. A full-grown plant makes a magnificent specimen.

Cultivation

DIFFICULTY Easy; virtually no input.

SOW in pots indoors or on a patio from mid-spring. For leaves you can make successional sowings (through the winter if indoors), but for seeds you need to start early and plant the seedlings out for a long season of growt h.

SPACE Seedlings to 10–15cm (4–6in) apart by removing a few from the pots; don't disturb the roots.

CARE Water sparingly in dry spells, but be careful as the plants dislike wet conditions.

STORAGE Cut the flowerheads when the seeds have formed and dry them upside down in a dry airy place. Put paper bags loosely over the heads to prevent any seed falling where you don't want it. Store the dried seeds in a screw-top glass jar until they're needed.

Keep it happy by…

Providing an open, sunny, well-drained growing site for your seed-producing specimens and grow leaf-producers in containers for best results.

Worth trying…

Dill (*Anethum graveolens*) – This is the species and the usual variety that is grown. It reaches 90cm (3ft) tall if it is allowed to flower and set seed.

'Mammoth' – This variety is grown specifically for seed production. It is less leafy and runs to seed early.

Enjoy it…

As soon as there is enough leaf to harvest. The plants can be used as a cut-and-come-again crop. Regrowth will occur, but sow a new batch of seeds once you are about halfway through the first for continuous supplies. Avoid using the leaves of seed plants if you want to avoid spoiling your garden display; the seeds form towards the end of the summer and can be collected straight off the plants.

Look out for…

The plants are susceptible to poor conditions – a wet, cold summer, or heavy, wet soil can spell disaster. Keep some indoors so that at least you get something, no matter what the weather is like.

Fennel

SOW APR, MAY, JUN, JUL
harvest MAY, JUN, JUL, AUG, SEP

This herb is quite like dill but a little more robust, producing taller (1.5–1.8m/5–6ft) cane-like stems of feathery leaves; it is an attractive addition to any garden, vegetable or decorative. The seeds and leaves are delicately aniseed flavoured. The leaves are traditionally used in fish cooking, and are also good with eggs and in salads, while fennel seeds are a necessity for many Indian and Middle Eastern dishes. A handful of fennel seeds are also good to chew as a breath freshener.

Like dill, fennel has feathery leaves, though they are somewhat darker and finer. The flat yellow flowerheads last throughout the summer months.

Cultivation

DIFFICULTY Easy; virtually no input.

SOW a few seeds in a pot in spring, thin them carefully and plant the whole clump without breaking up the rootball.

SPACE One plant will be plenty, give it at least 60cm (2ft) in each direction.

CARE Fennel needs little care apart from watering until it is established. At the end of autumn, cut down the stems to 2.5–5cm (1–2in) above the ground and the plants will re-grow next spring.

STORAGE Cut the flowerheads when the seeds have formed and dry them upside down in a dry airy place. Put paper bags loosely over the heads to prevent any seed falling where you don't want it. Store the dried seeds in a screw-top glass jar until they're needed.

Keep them happy by…

Raising them in a pot to begin with; although your own plants will self-seed like mad, bought seeds sown in the open don't do so well.

Worth trying…

Fennel (*Foeniculum vulgare*) – This is the usual green-leaved form with strong, feathery leaves and yellow cow-parsley-like flowers throughout summer and early autumn.

Bronze fennel (*Foeniculum vulgare purpureum*) – This has dark bronze-purple foliage and is excellent in decorative borders with tall plants such as common foxgloves and delphiniums, as well as pale pink roses. It self-seeds producing a mixture of purple-leaved and green-leaved seedlings.

Enjoy them…

As soon as the leaves are large enough. Use young leaves as these are most tender and have a better flavour.

Look out for…

Self-seeding is the only problem, so remove fading flowerheads if you don't want seeds to form.

Self-sown seedlings

If you don't deadhead your fennel, you will get abundant self-sown seedlings. If you want them, fine, if not, pull out unwanted ones while they are still tiny, otherwise their tap roots will break off when you pull and the plants will regrow.

Lemon grass

SOW FEB, MAR, APR, MAY
harvest YEAR-ROUND

A principal ingredient in Thai cooking, as well as other exotic cuisine, lemon grass is a somewhat coarse plant, capable of reaching 1.2m (4ft) high, with rough grassy leaves. A native of India, it is tender, so in the British winter it needs to be cosseted in the warm as a houseplant, although it will survive in a sheltered place outside over the summer. Keep it away from areas where young children play as the leaves are very sharp-edged – one of its other common names is barbed-wire grass.

Cultivation

DIFFICULTY Easy; low input.

SOW Indoors at room temperature in spring or early summer.

PLANT As an alternative to growing from seed, you can root a piece of bought lemon grass in a jam jar of water. Pot it up when the roots are 1cm (1½in) long, which won't take very long, except in winter.

SPACE Grow on in pots; two or three lemon grass plants will give you all you need.

CARE Keep the plants in a sunny situation; in winter they need a temperature of at least 13°C (55°F) or even warmer – room temperature. In summer, move them to a conservatory, where they are quite heat-tolerant if they are kept well watered, or put them out on a warm, sunny patio. Water generously, particularly in summer.

STORAGE The harvested stems stay fresh for some time in the fridge, or in a jar with their bases in about 2.5cm (1in) of water.

Keep them happy by...

Watering generously during hot dry weather. Repotting or dividing as the plants grow bigger.

Worth trying...

Lemon grass (*Cymbopogon citratus*) – This is the only form. It makes a dense clump of grassy leaves reaching 30cm (12in) across and 75cm (2½ft) high in a couple of years. It can be kept in check in a smaller pot, but will need plenty of regular feeding and watering to flourish.

Enjoy them...

As soon as the plants have developed slightly swollen, whitish stem bases – after about a year. The best way to harvest stems from an established plant is to divide the clump and replant one or two stems, keeping back what you need for the kitchen.

Look out for...

No problems, except for those sharp leaves.

The sleek but sharp-edged foliage of lemon grass.

Marjoram and oregano

SOW APR
plant MAY, JUN
harvest MAY, JUN, JUL, AUG, SEP

Marjoram and oregano both belong to the same genus – *Origanum* – and are similar in flavour, though oregano is usually more pungent. They are excellent combined with tomatoes, such as in pizza topping, and as a complementary flavouring for meat, particularly lamb; oregano is the main herb used in Greek salad. The bushy plants are easy to look after and are attractive with strongly aromatic leaves and tiny pink or white flowers which are loved by bees and butterflies.

Cultivation

DIFFICULTY Easy; very low input.
SOW thinly in pots on a windowsill indoors; plant out as potfuls rather than pricking out seedlings.
PLANT them out from mid-spring after the last frosts. As two or three plants will provide you with plenty of leaves, it is often simpler to buy them (cheaply) from garden centres and nurseries. This will also make it easier to grow several different varieties. Over the growing season, the sprawling stems often grow roots, and these roots can be removed to make new plants in midsummer.
SPACE Plant 23cm (9in) apart, or use them as decorative plants around the garden or in pots.
CARE Water in well, and water in very dry spells. Remove the dead flowerheads. Sweet marjoram does not survive the winter, so pull out old plants in late autumn. Leave perennials over winter, giving them a haircut in mid-spring.
STORAGE In a good growing season the leaves will contain plenty of aromatic oils and the best can be dried for storage in a screw-top glass jar.

Keep them happy by...

Providing them with a warm, sheltered growing position with plenty of sun and they will produce very aromatic leaves.

Worth trying...

Greek oregano (possibly as subspecies of *O. vulgare*) – This variety has bristly aromatic leaves and is the one for Mediterranean cookery and barbecues. It could do with winter protection as it is not reliably hardy.
Pot marjoram (*Origanum onites*) – This is the best for general use. It is an evergreen perennial, 30cm (12in) wide and high, with deep mauve flowers in midsummer, usually grown from cuttings.
Sweet or knotted marjoram (*Origanum majorana*) – This strongly aromatic, slightly floppy plant reaches about 30cm (12in) high and has clusters of tiny white flowers. It is grown as an annual.
Wild marjoram (*Origanum vulgare*) – Reaching 45cm (18in) high and wide, this small, evergreen, spreading plant has slightly hairy leaves and very small mauve flowers. It grows wild and is highly aromatic but does not develop a particularly strong flavour. The cultivar 'Aureum' has attractive golden leaves.

Enjoy them...

As soon as the plants have enough growth.

Look out for...

Poor growing conditions – cool weather and lots of rain – affect the strength of the flavour. Put some in well-drained pots on a sunny patio to recreate their baking homeland.

Wild marjoram (above left) and its golden-leaved variety 'Aureum' (above right) make pretty garden plants and are very popular with insects, particularly bees, but they aren't the best for cooking flavour.

Mint

plant APR, MAY, JUN
harvest MAY, JUN, JUL, AUG, SEP

Mint sauce with lamb and chopped mint on new potatoes, peas or broad beans are classic British uses of this herb, but it can do so much more besides: mint is excellent as a tea infusion, in flower arrangements (where it also acts as a fly repellent), and it also adds character to some Middle Eastern dishes. When well grown they are attractive plants with deliciously aromatic leaves.

Cultivation

DIFFICULTY Easy; will grow with no input, but better results come from harder work.

PLANT Buy young plants of named varieties from herb farms, nurseries or garden centres and plant them in humus-rich, fertile, moisture-retentive soil.

SPACE One plant of each of your favourite varieties is enough; allow 45cm (18in) between them. Mint can spread rapidly; to avoid this plant it in a largish bottomless container, such as an old bucket, sunk into the ground but with about 5cm (2in) of the rim showing.

CARE Water in new plants and water regularly in dry spells. Mulch and feed with a general-purpose fertilizer each spring when new growth first appears.

STORAGE The leaves can be dried for winter use but this is a herb best used fresh.

Keep it happy by...

Not cutting it back in midsummer. This has been traditional to encourage more leafy shoots, but, in fact, the flowers don't harm the plant in any way and they attract bees and butterflies, which is never a bad thing. When the flowers have faded, cut the flowered stems down to 5–7.5cm (2–3in) above ground and new shoots will soon appear.

Mint quickly exhausts the soil, so dig it up in spring every other year just as growth re-starts and replant one strong young section in a new site with freshly prepared ground.

Worth trying...

Apple mint (*Mentha suaveolens*) – This has large, slightly hairy, crinkly leaves and branching spikes of lilac flowers. The delicate flavour is good for mild mint sauce or jelly.

Eau de cologne mint (*Mentha* x *piperita* f. *citrata*) – Not surprisingly, the dark green, smooth leaves of this mint smell of eau de cologne. It's good with potatoes and peas, and is the very best variety for cutting for decoration.

Spearmint, or garden mint (*Mentha spicata*) – This is the commonest kind, with almost shiny, deep green leaves that have serrated edges, and mauve flowers. It's the best mint for mint sauce or to cook with new potatoes or peas.

Enjoy it...

As short sprigs as soon as the plants are growing well. You can continue harvesting throughout summer. Pot up some rooted stems or take 10cm (4in) cuttings in late summer for continued supplies of leaves over winter.

Look out for...

Mint falls prey to powdery mildew in mid- to late summer, just after it has flowered. Cut the plant to 5–7.5cm (2–3in) above the ground, feed and water it well and apply a 2.5cm (1in) mulch; strong new shoots should soon appear.

Mint rust produces small orange-red spots on the foliage. Pick off and destroy affected leaves.

Pineapple mint (*Mentha suaveolens* 'Variegata') looks unusual with its milky white variegation and has a good compact habit, but it lacks culinary virtues.

Parsley

SOW MAR, APR, MAY
harvest MAY, JUN, JUL, AUG, SEP, OCT

No kitchen garden is complete without parsley: plant it and find ways to use it, such as in stocks, sauces, as a traditional garnish, in potato salads, green salads and as a partial or total replacement for the basil in pesto sauce. The flat-leaved type is considered superior to the curly-leaved type in cooking, but this, as we all know, is excellent as a garnish. Parsley is best grown afresh each year as it runs to seed very quickly in its second season.

Cultivation

DIFFICULTY Easy; low input once it has germinated.
SOW Thinly where you want it to grow, or in small pots; plant these out without disturbing the rootball as parsley doesn't

transplant well. Thin in situ seedlings as necessary. Sow seeds in pots on the windowsill for a year-round indoor supply, every three months should be sufficient.
SPACE Thin plants to 15cm (6in) apart with 15cm (6in) between rows.
CARE Water regularly. Remove yellowing leaves. Replace plants when they seem 'tired' or if they start running to seed.
STORAGE It is really best eaten fresh, so keep those indoor pots going over winter. Alternatively, freeze it in bunches in plastic bags or chopped up and made into ice-cubes.

Keep it happy by…

Sowing in quite rich, moisture-retentive soil – parsley is greedy. Feed the plants every few weeks using a general-purpose liquid or soluble feed. This ensures that they grow strongly with that rich green colouring and flavour.

Worth trying…

Flat-leaved parsley – This is the non-frilly, flat-leaved type, which is sometimes called French or Italian parsley. It makes bushy plants of about 30cm (12in) high, with deeply serrated and shiny leaflets.
'Lisette' – An improved curly-leaved variety with clouds of leaves on plants reaching 60cm (24in).
'Moss Curled' – The favourite curly-leaved variety, with rich green very frilly leaves on short plants.

Enjoy it…

As individual leaves, removed complete with stalks, as soon as they are large enough. Choose good specimens, leaving behind the youngest and oldest.

Look out for…

Seed germination can be very slow. Low temperature is almost always the problem. Try a pot indoors in temperatures above 16°C (60°F). Thin them slightly if necessary and pot on the whole clump.

Bolting will occur when you least want it to happen. Sow regularly to always have a fresh supply.

'Moss Curled' parsley is the one we Brits tend to favour, and for good reason: it has a lovely rich colour and very good flavour.

Rosemary

SOW APR, MAY, JUN, JUL
harvest APR, MAY, JUN, JUL, AUG, SEP, OCT

Rosemary leaves are wonderful for flavouring roast potatoes, vegetables and meat, particularly lamb; they are widely used in Mediterranean cooking and salad dressings, and a few sprigs chucked on barbeque coals will fill the air with fragrance. Beside all this, the shrubby plants with their blue flowers make a decorative contribution to any garden and some varieties can survive and produce their highly aromatic leaves in the least promising conditions, even in a shady, north-facing spot in milder areas, though they do prefer something warmer.

Cultivation

DIFFICULTY Easy; very low input.

PLANT As a young potted specimen, readily bought from herb farms, nurseries or garden centres, in a warm sheltered spot with well-drained soil. One or two will be enough, unless you want to make a low hedge.

SPACE Allow 60–90cm (2–3ft) between rosemary and its neighbours; if you are planning a low hedge of rosemary, 30cm (12in) is adequate.

CARE Water new plants in and keep them watered in dry spells until they are well established.

STORAGE If you aren't too greedy, you should be able to pick leaves throughout the year. However, rosemary does store well: when you prune or clip the plants, save the tips (about 15cm/6in long) to dry. Wash them then dip them for a second or two in boiling water followed by cold water. Hang them in small bunches away from sunlight.

Keep it happy by…

Trimming plants in midsummer after the first flush of flowers. Remove long straggly branches to prevent splitting at the base.

Worth trying…

Common rosemary (*Rosmarinus officinalis*) – This is the widely available species and it reaches 90cm (3ft) or more high and wide; it's attractive in the garden and good for culinary use. Prostratus Group (also known as *R. lavandulaceus*) – This compact, low-spreading rosemary is slightly less hardy than other kinds. It has light blue flowers and highly aromatic leaves that aren't the best for cooking. It can be clipped formally and is

'Miss Jessopp's Upright' – As the name suggests, this version is tall and vertical, perhaps reaching 1.5m (5ft) high; it has pale violet flowers speckled with deeper blue. It is good for training as a mid-height hedge.

good in a pot by the kitchen door or even in a hanging basket. 'Severn Sea' – This is a smaller, mound-shaped plant, more or less 75cm (2½ft) high and wide.
'Tuscan Blue' – An upright type with dark blue flowers.

Enjoy it…

As sprigs when the plants are large enough. The shrubs are evergreen, so you can cut for cooking at any time of year, though the flavour is most intense during the growing season.

Look out for…

Rosemary has few problems but a recent invader from the continent, rosemary beetle, is proving to be a pest, mainly in south-east England but also in other parts of Britain. The beetles are small, oval, metallic-green with purple stripes and they eat the foliage of rosemary and other Mediterranean herbs, especially lavender, thyme and sage. At present, there's no chemical deterrent to protect plants against rosemary beetle, so pick them off by hand.

Sage

plant APR, MAY, JUN, JUL
harvest APR, MAY, JUN, JUL, AUG, SEP, OCT

With its soft leaves in green, purple or variegated with white, sage is an attractive garden plant as well as being the traditional ingredient in stuffing. Don't limit yourself to using it with onions, its talents are much more varied: butters, sauces, breads, in place of a bay leaf in almost any dish and with vegetables as well as meat.

Cultivation

DIFFICULTY Easy; low input.

PLANT Young specimens – easily purchased from garden centres and herb farms – in a sunny and sheltered spot with well-drained soil.

SPACE You'll only need one culinary variety but allow 60cm (2ft) between it and it's neighbours. Ornamental sages need less space – 45cm (18in) will do.

CARE Water in new plants; once established, sage is fairly drought tolerant. Prune plants in spring to tidy their shape.

STORAGE Pick perfect leaves in summer, dip them briefly into boiling water then cold, and lay them out thinly on baking sheets to dry in the airing cupboard or another dark, warm, dry place. Store them in screw-top glass jars.

Common sage is capable of making huge mounds of soft sage-green foliage. It makes a wonderful garden plant as well as a good culinary herb.

Replacement cuttings

Take cuttings, 10cm (4in) long, from the tips of strong, healthy stems in early summer. Remove the lower leaves. Fill a 10cm (4in) pot with a mix of half and half potting grit and multipurpose compost and insert up to five cuttings. Stand the pots indoors out of direct sun. Pot them in late summer and keep under cover for the first winter.

Keep it happy by…

Giving it plenty of time to get established before winter sets in. It is hardy, but will do better this way. Take cuttings of older plants (5 or 6 years old) in late spring or early summer to ensure you always have some sage (*see* box).

Worth trying…

Common sage (*Salvia officinalis*) – This is a wide and low, bushy plant 60cm (2ft) high and 90cm (3ft) wide. Its heavily aromatic leaves are soft, textured and grey-green; the purple-blue flowers attract bees.

Golden sage (*Salvia officinalis* 'Icterina') – This attractive sage grows to 45cm (18in) high and has gold and light green leaf variegation. It is quite a strong grower and is good for cooking and in flower arrangements.

Purple sage (*Salvia officinalis* 'Purpurascens') – Smaller than the species at 45cm (18in) high and a little wider, this has wonderful purple-grey leaves that are just as good for cooking, and purplish flowers.

Tricolor sage (*Salvia officinalis* 'Tricolor') – Although pretty with its mauve, cream and green variegated leaves and blue-toned flowers, this sage is slow and its growth is fairly weak. It is better as an ornamental and in flower arrangements than for cooking and is likely to succumb to winter wet if you don't have it in ideal growing conditions; take cuttings just in case.

Enjoy it…

As soon as the plants are large enough not to miss a few leaves. It is best from early spring to autumn, after which the leaves wither and are not pleasant to use. Dry some for winter.

Look out for…

Sage suffers from attack by rosemary beetle (*see* page 129).

Wet weather can kill off some stems. Old sage bushes tend to flop open and the central thick woody stems don't produce new leaves. As a last resort, cut them back hard in spring, or just prune regularly in spring so as to avoid needing to do this.

Thyme

plant APR, MAY, JUN, JUL
harvest YEAR ROUND

There is an enormous range of thyme cultivars and
many are ornamental as well as culinary. It's fun to make
a collection, but bear in mind that some aren't really
very useful for cooking. As an added bonus bees love
the flowers, which appear from early to midsummer.
In the kitchen thyme is one of the traditional ingredients
of bouquet garni and its strongly aromatic flavour adds
zing to breads, stuffings, stews, risottos and a variety of
fish and meat dishes.

Cultivation

DIFFICULTY Easy, when grown in the right conditions;
low input.

PLANT Pots of thyme plants are easily and cheaply bought at
garden centres and herb farms. Plant them in a sunny spot with
poor, very well-drained soil.

SPACE Bushy, upright types 23cm (9in) apart, but allow 30cm
(12in) for spreading varieties.

CARE Water in and provide water during very dry weather while
they are establishing themselves; after this, watering is rarely
necessary. Give plants a trim to improve their shape and remove
any dead stems in spring. Take cuttings to replace plants every
third year (*see* rosemary, page 129, but make the cuttings smaller)
from midsummer to early autumn.

STORAGE Dry surplus thyme in summer, but not when it's
flowering. Dip whole stems briefly in boiling water then cold water,
then hang them upside down to dry in an airy place out of direct
sunlight. When perfectly dry, rub the leaves off the stems with your
fingers and store them in screw-top jars in a cool, dark place.

Keep them happy by…

Providing really poor, really well-drained soil. Use lots of grit to
make it that way, or grow them in raised beds or containers in a
half and half mixture of John Innes No.1 and potting grit. Don't
feed them; they like it tough. Plant them early in the growing
season, as even though thyme is a hardy perennial, the plants
will find it easier to survive if they are well established by winter.

Worth trying…

Caraway thyme (*Thymus herba-barona*) – A very low, creeping
species only 5cm (2in) or so high, spreading up to 30cm (12in),

Common or garden thyme (*Thymus vulgaris*) is a
mound-forming thyme, reaching about 30cm (12in) high
and two-thirds as wide. This popular culinary thyme has
dark green narrow leaves with a strong flavour and aroma,
and dark mauve-pink flowers.

with caraway-scented shiny green leaves and delicate
rose-purple flowers.

Lemon thyme (*Thymus* x *citriodorus*) – This is a diminutive bushy
plant, 15cm (6in) high with a mild lemony flavour. 'Aureus' has
yellow leaves.

Orange thyme (*Thymus* x *citriodorus* 'Fragrantissimus') – This
thyme's small grey leaves are strongly orange scented; its
flowers are pale pink or white and appear in June/July; good for
putting under duck while it's roasting.

Thymus x *citriodorus* 'Bertram Anderson' – This is a spreading,
dual-purpose variety – good for cooking and ornament. It is
10cm (4in) high but up to 60cm (2ft) wide, with mildly lemon-
flavoured, gold-variegated leaves and mauve-pink flowers.

Enjoy them…

As short shoot tips when the plants are well established.
Regular harvesting ensures you get plenty of new shoots to cut.
Thymes can be picked all year round, though the warm sun of
summer produces the best flavours.

Look out for…

They are sensitive to unsuitable growing conditions. Too much
wet will cause their demise, particularly through the winter, and
avoid humus-rich soil at all costs.

Season by season

Like most forms of gardening, growing vegetables is about patience and waiting. This isn't to say that you can't achieve some things quickly and do some things instantly, but the reality is that most crops take their time and won't be hurried (or not by much). Many gardeners would say that this is the attraction of gardening, along with the way it puts you in touch with the seasons. Here is an overview of each of the four seasons, showing what you need to do at the different times of year to ensure healthy and productive plants.

The vegetable gardening year

Even on and around this small island, weather conditions can vary greatly between the north and south, east and west, making a difference of up to three weeks in the start and end of the seasons. This is most noticeable in spring, as the trees in some areas come into leaf well ahead of those in others, and frosts can still be a threat in some places long after they have disappeared from milder counties. For this reason, the calendar months are not always the most accurate indicators of when to schedule key events, such as sowing, planting out and expecting to harvest; however, they are the most commonly recognized and so have been used here. This book assumes that spring starts in March, summer in June, autumn in September and winter in December, which gives a good general idea, but you should make adjustments based on what you know happens where you live. With experience, such weather judgements will become more accurate and you will achieve greater success in your vegetable growing along with an enormous sense of satisfaction.

The autumn season

The vegetable gardener's year never really begins or ends, as there is always something growing, always something to be harvested and always something that could be done, but, if pressed, you could say the cycle starts in the autumn with the preparation of the ground for next year's crop (*see* pages 32–5).

Autumn is a great time to be out in the garden, enjoying the last of the sunshine, taking stock of your successes and failures and making plans for next year. Make the most of the cooler weather to tidy up used ground and dig in compost or manure. This work is very satisfying and you might even look forward to some rain to encourage the worms to start working on the organic material, mixing it into your soil. You can still be harvesting late vegetables and looking forward to new crops, too.

From digging to staking, planting to harvesting, there are always jobs to be done in the vegetable garden. On a sunny autumn day it's good to have a reason to get outside and have a potter round.

Early autumn

Now is the time to start thinking about clearing the ground for a new vegetable bed (see pages 32–3). You can do the work any time until late autumn if the weather is favourable. Towards the end of the month, remember to cover late outdoor crops with fleece at night if it turns cold. If you haven't got a greenhouse but do have a conservatory, move tender plants, such as aubergines and peppers, into it to ripen any remaining fruit.

■ **Last chance to ...** Ripen tomatoes. Remove the lower leaves and growing tips of indoor tomatoes to encourage green fruit to swell and ripen.

Swiss chard and perpetual spinach still going strong in a large walled garden. On the far side of espaliered apple trees, late ornamentals, including dahlias, add a splash of colour.

Sow **Indoors:** Rocket for a windowsill crop. **Under cover:** Peas (mangetout), salad leaves (various), turnips (early autumn). **Outside:** Onions (winter-hardy spring), spinach (spring/autumn varieties), salad leaves (various).

Plant out Cabbages (spring-hearting), onion sets (overwintering varieties).

Harvest **Under cover:** Aubergines, beans (French dwarf), chillies, cucumbers, peppers (green as well as red), tomatoes. **Outside:** Artichokes (globe), aubergines, beans (French dwarf, flageolet, haricot, runner), beetroot, broccoli (summer-sprouting), Brussels sprouts (early varieties), cabbages (summer- and autumn-hearting, red), calabrese, carrots (maincrop), cauliflowers (summer- and autumn-heading), celeriac, celery, chillies, courgettes, cucumbers, endive, Florence fennel, kohl rabi, leeks (baby and early varieties), marrows, onions (summer varieties and spring), peas (mangetout, sugar snap, shelling), peppers, potatoes (second early and maincrop), radishes (summer and winter), salad leaves (various), spinach (spring/autumn varieties, New Zealand, perpetual), squashes (summer), swedes, sweetcorn, Swiss chard, tomatoes, turnips.

Mid-autumn

Eke out late tender outdoor crops, such as courgettes and salads, by protecting them with fleece on cold nights and during the day if it is chilly. Do the same with greenhouse

Don't forget

In autumn your compost heap will be growing in size as you clear veg beds. If you feel the need to turn it, do be careful of disturbing hibernating slow worms. This goes for earlier in the year, too – around May and June – when they use a warm heap as an incubator for their eggs.

crops by closing the vents and door early in the afternoon to trap more warmth overnight. After harvesting the last tomatoes, peppers and aubergines towards the end of the season, pull out the plants and clean up the greenhouse, remove any shading and work well-rotted organic matter into the soil border before sowing winter crops.

■ **Stake Brussels sprouts and sprouting broccoli** Use sturdy stakes to keep them upright in windy weather. This is especially important if your vegetable garden is on an exposed site.

■ **Last chance to ...** Dig in organic matter. If this is not done now, it won't be fully incorporated by the time you want to plant in spring. Remember, don't add it to beds that are intended for root crops next year.

Sow **Under cover:** Peas (mangetout), salad leaves (lamb's lettuce). **Outside:** Onions (winter-hardy spring), salad leaves (lamb's lettuce).

Plant out Cabbages (spring-hearting), onion sets (overwintering varieties).

Harvest **Under cover:** Aubergines, beans (French dwarf), chillies, cucumbers, salad leaves (various), tomatoes, turnips. **Outside:** Artichokes (Jerusalem), beans (flageolet, haricot, runner), beetroot, broccoli (summer-sprouting), Brussels sprouts (early varieties), cabbages (summer- and autumn-hearting, red), carrots (maincrop and early varieties), cauliflowers

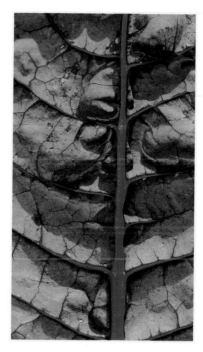

Ruby chard is a decorative addition to the vegetable garden and looks particularly magnificent towards the end of the growing season, when its leaves are lit by the low autumn sun.

(summer- and autumn-heading), celeriac, celery, chicory/radicchio (hearting varieties), courgettes, endive, leeks (early varieties), marrows, parsnips, peas (shelling, early varieties), potatoes (maincrop and new from specially prepared seed potatoes), pumpkins, radishes (summer and winter), salad leaves (various), spinach (spring/autumn varieties, New Zealand, perpetual), squashes (summer and autumn), swedes, Swiss chard, tomatoes.

The winter season

Gone are the days when winter was a quiet time for gardeners. Nowadays, autumn-like weather seems to extend late into the calendar year, while spring can come early, so it is often possible to continue digging and preparing the beds on and off throughout winter. However, when the weather gets really cold and wet it is nicer to be indoors fine-tuning plans for next year's crops.

On pleasant days there are plenty of other jobs to be done around about, such as tidying the shed, cleaning pots in preparation for spring sowing and checking over your stored harvest for signs of rot or rodent damage, and you can still be nipping outside to harvest a wide variety of fresh vegetables.

Late autumn to early spring

While you can still be sowing various salad leaves under cover and for windowsill crops, as well as lifting roots for forcing chicory (*see* page 82), late autumn and early winter are generally quite quiet as far as planting goes. Come midwinter, however, and the possibilities begin to increase. It is then that you can start to chit early seed potatoes to produce a very early crop under cover and also sow summer-heading cauliflower seeds indoors.

■ **First chance to ...** Get seeds in. In late winter sow seeds of aubergines, chillies, peppers and tomatoes in pots in the warmth indoors (at room temperature) to give you the earliest plants for growing under glass.

Winter is a fine time for lovers of forced chicory, which comes into its own now, as long as you remembered to start it off in the autumn.

It is well worth the effort of cleaning and oiling garden tools before you put them away for the winter.

Sow

Indoors: Cauliflowers (summer-heading varieties) in mid- and late winter, and sow salad leaves (lamb's lettuce) from late autumn–early spring.

■ **Chit potatoes** from midwinter to early spring, starting with very early varieties for under cover and ending with second earlies for planting outside.

Plant Outside (late winter–early spring): Garlic, if you forgot to do it in late autumn.

Harvest Under cover (late autumn–early winter): Salad leaves (various, including lamb's lettuce and rocket), turnips.

Don't forget

Garlic is best planted outdoors in late autumn to give it a long growing season and to be sure of good-sized cloves at harvesting time.

Harvest

Outside (mid-autumn–early spring): Artichokes (Jerusalem), broccoli (sprouting), Brussels sprouts, cabbages (winter-hearting and Savoy), carrots (maincrop), cauliflowers (summer-, autumn- and winter-heading), celeriac, chicory (hearting), endive, kale, leeks (early and late varieties), onions, parsnips, potatoes (new, maincrop), radishes (summer and winter), salad leaves (various, including lamb's lettuce and rocket), spinach (spring/autumn varieties, spinach (perpetual), swedes, Swiss chard.

The spring season

Along with farmers and fishermen, gardeners can always sense when spring comes, and it has nothing to do with a specific date. When was the weather ever that predictable? No, it's more to do with a feeling in the air outside, an increase (albeit slight) in ambient temperatures, and a sense of imminent growth. This feeling gives us an energy boost, which is a good thing because from mid- to late spring and early summer you could easily fill every waking hour in the vegetable garden. There is so much planting, potting up, transplanting, tying in and training to be done. It's a good thing (and, of course, no coincidence) that longer evenings come with the warmer weather.

A beautifully turned out vegetable garden in mid-spring. Tulips provide a colourful backdrop and the rows of vegetables are full of promise.

Early spring

It is time to complete the digging of the vegetable beds. Ideally, you will have dug in organic matter last autumn; it's a bit late to do it now, but you could if it is very well rotted and in beds you aren't going to use instantly. Prepare ground for sowing and planting (*see* pages 32–6), then get down to the business of sowing – it'll keep you busy.

■ **Last chance to …** Chit seed potatoes. First and second earlies do better when chitted (*see* page 102); maincrops don't need chitting.

Sow **Indoors in warmth:** Aubergines, beans (broad, dwarf, French), Brussels sprouts (early varieties), cauliflowers (autumn-heading), celeriac, celery, chillies, peas (early mangetout varieties), peppers, salad leaves (various), tomatoes. **Outside under cover:** Artichokes (globe), broccoli (summer-sprouting), calabrese, peas (mangetout), radish, salad leaves (various), spinach (summer varieties), turnips. **Outside:** Beetroot (early varieties), Brussels sprouts, cabbages (summer- and early-autumn-hearting, red), calabrese, carrots (early varieties), leeks, onions (spring), parsnips, peas (shelling, early varieties), radishes, salad leaves (various), spinach (summer varieties).

Plant out **Under cover:** Potatoes (earlies). **Outside:** Artichokes (globe, Jerusalem), cauliflowers (summer-heading), garlic, onion sets, potatoes (earlies, end of early spring), shallots.

Harvest **Under cover:** Lamb's lettuce, peas (mangetout). **Outside:** Broccoli (sprouting), cauliflowers (winter-heading), endive, kale, leeks (late varieties).

Decorative plants

Now is the time to sow the seed of annual flowers. Why not plant some flowers that you can eat, such as nasturtium (*Tropaeolum majus*), borage (*Borago officinalis*) and pot marigold (*Calendula officinalis*)? Many annuals can be sown in situ, or you can raise them in pots to plant out later. If you like wandering around the veg patch in the early evening, grazing on the odd pea pod here and spinach leaf there, grow some night-scented stock (*Matthiola bicornis*). The flowers of this little plant shrivel up during the day and open at dusk, emitting the most wonderful, sweet dolly mixture smell.

Mid-spring

If we're lucky, mid-spring can be warm with plenty of rain to get the crops going; if we're not, it can be cold and dry – not the thing for young seedlings. Weed seeds care less about the weather and will be romping away all over the bare earth of the vegetable garden. Do as much hoeing as you can to keep everything under control and help your youngsters to emerge. If slugs are a problem, purchase biological controls (*see* page 53) for use towards the end of the month – they have a use-by date and are best applied during warm damp weather, so you need to time your ordering carefully.

■ **First chance to …** Start hardening off tender vegetables. In mild areas, hardening off of tomatoes, runner beans and so on can begin.

Sow **Indoors in warmth:** Aubergines, beans (French climbing and dwarf, flageolet and haricot, runner), courgettes, cucumbers (for indoors and out), Florence fennel, marrows, peppers, pumpkins, squashes (summer and autumn),

sweetcorn, tomatoes. **Outside under cover:** Artichokes (globe), salad leaves (pak choi). **Outside:** Beans (broad), beetroot, broccoli, Brussels sprouts, cabbages (summer-, autumn- and winter-hearting, Savoy, red), calabrese, carrot (maincrop), cauliflowers (winter-heading), kale, kohl rabi, leeks (baby and normal), onions (spring), peas (mangetout, sugar

Plant leeks using a large dibber and then 'puddle' each plant in by filling the hole with water.

snap, shelling), radishes, salad leaves (various), spinach (summer varieties, New Zealand, perpetual), Swiss chard, turnips.

Plant out

Under cover (mid-spring): Beans (French dwarf), tomatoes.
Outside: Artichokes (globe), asparagus, beans (broad), broccoli (summer-sprouting), calabrese, cauliflowers (summer- and autumn-heading), onion sets, potatoes (earlies first, then second earlies, then maincrop).

Harvest

Under cover: Peas (mangetout, autumn-sown), salad leaves (various), spinach (baby leaves from summer varieties).
Outside: Asparagus (mid-spring), cabbages (spring-hearting), cauliflowers (winter-heading), kale,

spinach (baby leaves from summer varieties, mid-spring).

Late spring

This is a fantastic time, when the current season's plants grow head and shoulders above the weeds and the vegetable garden looks lush and full of promise. Weeding is still necessary, though, and this is when other unwanted visitors may arrive. Watch out for greenfly and blackfly – if your plants are healthy and the infestation is not great, the wildlife in your garden should be able to keep on top of them; otherwise, *see* pages 52–5.

Don't be too impatient to plant out tender plants. If the weather is cool you won't lose anything by waiting a week or two. With aubergines, chillies and peppers, wait until late in the season, or even into early summer, as frost is a killer.

A cold frame works very hard in spring and early summer. Always harden off young plants before planting them out.

Don't forget

Sow salad leaves, radishes and other crops on a little-and-often basis – schedule it in as a weekly 'must-do' job.

The summer season

After the frenetic activity of spring, summer is a quieter time, although for the more energetic gardener there is no shortage of things to be done. Successional planting (*see* page 43) comes into its own now and is easily overlooked amid the rush of harvest – mark it on the calendar so you don't forget. Gluts can make you feel guilty, when you simply can't bear the thought of runner beans and courgettes for the fourth night in a row. If you can't give excess produce away, you could always experiment with preserving and freezing; if all else fails, chuck it on the compost heap – life's too short to fret and that way it can at

least make a contribution to next year's harvest.

Early summer

Vegetable plants work really hard during early summer and need plenty of water and food. This is the time when unexpected dry spells can check plants and spoil whole crops, so don't be tempted to bypass watering. Even on days when it has rained, check the soil to ensure it has been dampened thoroughly. Make container- and

Make good use of all the available space by catch-cropping fast-growing salad or veg between rows of other varieties. Marking out the row makes it easier to sow in a straight line.

Greenhouses and polytunnels

As the sun becomes stronger, fix up or paint on greenhouse shading to prevent the crops inside scorching, and damp down on hot days by watering all the surfaces, including the floor and the staging. This is best done in the morning and evening, and at midday if necessary. With polytunnels, the condensation that forms on the inside does both these jobs naturally, but do remember to open the ends for ventilation.

greenhouse-watering a daily task, if you haven't already been doing it through late spring. Greenhouse and container crops will have started to run out of the feed that was incorporated at planting time, so give them a regular liquid feed, too.

■ **Last chance to …** Sow swedes. Go on – give this old-fashioned root vegetable a well-deserved second chance.

Sow **Outside:** Beans (French climbing and dwarf, flageolet, haricot, runner), beetroot, carrots

(maincrop), chicory, endive, kale, kohl rabi, leeks (baby), onions (spring), peas (mangetout, sugar snap, early shelling, maincrop shelling), radishes, salad leaves (various), spinach (New Zealand, perpetual), swedes, sweetcorn, Swiss chard, turnips.

Plant out **Under cover:** Aubergines, chillies, peppers. **Outside:** Aubergines, beans (flageolet, haricot, runner), broccoli, Brussels sprouts, cabbages (summer- and autumn-hearting, red), calabrese, cauliflowers (winter-heading), celeriac, celery, chillies, courgettes, cucumbers, Florence fennel, kale, leeks, marrows, peppers, pumpkins, squashes (summer and autumn), tomatoes.

Harvest **Under cover:** Beans (French dwarf), Florence fennel, peas (mangetout), peppers (still green), potatoes (earlies), turnips. **Outside:** Asparagus, beans (broad, French dwarf), broccoli (summer-sprouting), calabrese, carrots (early varieties), cauliflowers (summer-heading), courgettes, garlic (autumn-planted), leeks (baby), marrows, onions (overwintering varieties and spring), peas (mangetout, sugar snap, early shelling), potatoes (first and second earlies), radishes, salad leaves (various), spinach (summer varieties, New Zealand), squashes (summer), turnips.

Midsummer

Continue with the daily watering and weekly (or fortnightly) feeding of crops in containers and under cover. As some successional and early crops come to an end, clear the ground and prepare it for more vegetables. It is always worth making a note of what has done well and where, for next year's planning. If you've been trying out new varieties, give them a score and decide whether to grow them again next year or experiment with something else.

■ **Last chance to…** Sow French dwarf beans and shelling peas: If you sow early shelling pea varieties you could be eating them into mid-autumn; the French dwarf beans will last into early autumn in a cold greenhouse.

Sow (outside) Beans (French dwarf), carrots (early varieties), chicory, endive, onions (spring), peas (early shelling), radishes

The first crop of runner beans is always exciting. Pick them while they're young and tender and keep picking to ensure production continues.

(summer and winter), salad leaves (various), spinach (perpetual), Swiss chard, turnips.

Plant (outside) Broccoli (sprouting), cabbages (winter-hearting, Savoy), Florence fennel, kale, potatoes (new from specially prepared seed potatoes).

Harvest **Under cover:** Aubergines, chillies, cucumbers, Florence fennel, peppers (still green), tomatoes. **Outside:** Artichokes (globe), aubergines, beans (broad, French climbing and dwarf, runner), beetroot, broccoli (summer-sprouting), calabrese, carrots (early varieties), cauliflowers (summer-heading), chillies, courgettes, cucumbers, garlic, kohl rabi, leeks (baby), marrows, onions

Keep on top of de-sideshooting tomatoes, they'll be growing at a great rate now and it's important not to let them grow foliage at the expense of fruit.

(overwintering and spring), peas (mangetout, sugar snap, early and maincrop shelling), potatoes (first and second earlies), radishes, salad leaves (various), shallots, spinach (New Zealand, perpetual), squashes (summer), sweetcorn, Swiss chard, tomatoes, turnips.

Late summer
Water, water, water – if you are going away make sure you organize holiday watering (*see* page 46); don't hope that it will rain. If you ask a friend or neighbour to do the job, tell them to help themselves to any crops that become ready; that way you don't come home to monstrous courgettes and stringy beans with no hope of new ones – you might also convert someone else to veg growing. Continue liquid feeding to keep container and under cover plants on tip-top form.

At the end of the month, remove lower leaves from outdoor tomato plants and nip out the growing tips at the top of each plant to encourage green fruit to swell and ripen before the end of the season.

■ It's not too late to … Get some new seeds in. Sow carrots and turnips now and protect the seedlings with fleece for fresh roots in mid- to late autumn.

Sow **Under cover:** Carrots (early varieties), salad leaves (various, including pak choi), turnips. **Outside:** Carrots (early varieties), onions (overwintering varieties and winter-hardy spring), radishes, salad leaves (various), spinach (spring/autumn varieties).

Under cover, cucumbers come thick and fast through summer. Check regularly under the large leaves as the fruits are often well hidden.

Plant out **Under cover:** Beans (French dwarf). **Outside:** Potatoes (new from specially prepared seed potatoes).

Harvest **Under cover:** Aubergines, chillies, cucumbers, peppers (green and red now), tomatoes. **Outside:** Artichokes (globe), aubergines, beans (French climbing and dwarf, runner), beetroot, broccoli (summer-sprouting), cabbages (spring-, summer- and autumn-hearting, red), calabrese, cauliflowers (summer- and autumn-heading), celery, chillies, courgettes, cucumbers, Florence fennel, garlic, kohl rabi, leeks (baby), marrows, onions (bulb and spring), peas (mangetout, sugar snap, maincrop shelling), peppers (green), potatoes (second earlies), radishes (summer and winter), salad leaves (various), shallots, spinach (New Zealand, perpetual), squashes (summer), sweetcorn, Swiss chard, tomatoes, turnips.

Index

Acknowledgements

BBC Books and OutHouse would like to thank the following for their assistance in preparing this book: Andrew McIndoe for his advice and guidance; Joanne Forrest Smith for picture research; Helena Caldon for proofreading; June Wilkins for the index.

Picture credits

Key t = top, b = bottom, l = left, r = right, c = centre

DK Images 33

GAP Photos Elke Borkowski 59. FhF Greenmedia 75. Marcus Harpur 42. Michael Howes 72. Lynn Keddie 85t. Zara Napier 41. Rice/ Buckland 58. Graham Strong 53

The Garden Collection Derek St Romaine 76. Nicola Stocken Tomkins 131

Garden World Images Trevor Sims 114

Sue Gordon 57bl, 65r, 104r

Andrew McIndoe 12t, 15cr, 43, 44c, 73, 84, 96b, 102, 105

Photolibrary David Askham 117. **Photolibrary/Fresh Food Images** Janet Bligh 85b

Robin Whitecross 37br, 40t, 40b, 44l, 52t, 80, 81, 93, 101, 106t, 106b, 111

Thanks are also due to the following designers and owners whose gardens appear in the book:

Rosemary Alexander, Stoneacre, Kent 12br. Darina Allen, Ballymaloe Cookery School, Co. Cork, Ireland 9, 53r, 137t. Audley End, Essex 25. Janet Bonney 22t. Tommaso del Buono & Paul Gazerwitz, RHS Chelsea Flower Show 2008 19b, 122. Rose Gray, The River Cafe, London 118. Robin Green & Ralph Cade 10. Bunny Guinness 11t. Christopher Lloyd, Great Dixter, East Sussex 26r. The Lodge, Slindon, Hampshire 110t. Sarah Raven, Perch Hill, East Sussex 19t, 58t, 60, 77, 87, 88, 94t, 98, 100r, 136. Gill Siddell 14b. Sue & Wol Staines, Glen Chantry, Essex 5r, 15t. Sarah Wain & Jim Buckland, West Dean Gardens, West Sussex 44r, 134. Sue Ward, Ladywood, Hampshire 30t. Kim Wilde & Richard Lucas, RHS Chelsea Flower Show 2005 30b. Adam Woolcott & Jonathan Swift, Chelsea Flower Show 2007 42. Helen Yemm, Ketley's, East Sussex 11b.